# SIGILS FOR MAGIC

## TECHNIQUES OF TRANSFORMATION

JONATHAN ARGENTO

# SIGILS FOR MAGIC

## TECHNIQUES OF TRANSFORMATION

BY

JONATHAN ARGENTO

PUBLISHED BY Fenix Flames Publishing Ltd 2023

Copyright © 2023   Jonathan Argento

All rights reserved including the right of reproduction in whole or in part in any form. No reproduction, copy or transmission of this publication may be made without written permission. No paragraph of this publication may be reproduced, copied or transmitted save with written permission or in accordance with the provisions of the Copyright Act 1956 (as amended). Any person who performs any unauthorised act in relation to this publication may be liable to criminal prosecution and civil claims for damages. The moral rights of the author have been asserted.

All names have been changed, except in those cases where individuals are already publicly known.

Published by Fenix Flames Publishing Ltd

Design & Layout: Ashley Mortimer
Cover Design: Jonathan Argento

Printed by Lightning Source International / Ingram Spark

Paperback  ISBN  978-1-913768-16-4
eBook  ISBN  978-1-913768-17-1

www.publishing.fenixflames.co.uk

# ACKNOWLEDGEMENTS

*Dedicated to the memory of Maureen Wheeler.*

Special thanks to Angela for all her support, and my sons and grandsons for all the joy they bring me. To all members and associates of the Wickham Coven, Lyceum, Astralis and Star Circle - we have walked this path together.

Many thanks to Merlyn and Cath for their unwavering support and valued guidance, Janet Farrar, and Gavin Bone for their wealth of knowledge, friendship, and the continuation of the legacy of Maureen Wheeler. To Vikki Bramshaw, whose friendship and insightful authorship always inspires me.

Thank you to all the organisers who are kind enough to ask me to speak at their events, the Witchfest crew, Baz and Max Cilla, Cazi Brook, Pia Morgan, Elric Sullivan, Mathew Callow, Julie Aspinall and the Coven of Gaia, Diane Narraway and Clan Dolmen.

Huge thanks to Angela Barker and Ashley Mortimer and all at Fenix Flames Publishing.

Lastly, my heartfelt thanks to Kerry Williams.

# Contents

Introduction     ix

1. Little Squiggles for Success ........... 1
2. Monograms of Thought ................. 11
3. Seashore Sigils ............................... 21
4. Sonorous Sorcery .......................... 29
5. Dot-to-dot Sudoku ........................ 37
6. Money sigils –
   Cash from Chaos Magic? .............. 47
7. Sigils for Protection ...................... 55
8. Intention and Ethics in Magic....... 63
9. Further Techniques ...................... 71
10. How does Magic Work? .............. 81
11. Sigils as Portals ............................. 87
12. Trance Sigils .................................. 97
13. Crossroads Sigils ........................... 105
14. Sigils as Sentient Beings ............... 113

Bibliography     121

# Introduction

Sigils are my favourite technique for creating change. They are simple, effective, easy to create and don't require a particular set of beliefs. Sigils are accessible to everyone.

Ancient sigils featured in the emergence of human consciousness. Recently, psychology has observed the way symbols speak to the conscious and unconscious mind. Studies in semiotics have recognised the global application of universal symbols, from logos and brands, to emojis and emoticons and the written and verbal use of puns and metaphors, now recognised as valid forms of communication. Sigils have always been a feature of human experience, irrespective of cultural setting.

The title *Sigils for Magic* reflects the increasing interest in sigils and magic in general within broader culture and a diffusion of these ideas, perhaps meeting a deeper need for change and re-enchantment within society. Modern sigil magic reflects a *bricolage*, or 'mash-up' of mixed media, redefining and drawing upon both arcane practice and contemporary culture.

Magic is concerned with creating change on both a personal and social level. Both expressions are valid, however, the former without the later, threatens to reduce magic to mere self-indulgence.

Historically, the idea of, or perhaps fear of magic, threatened the status quo of ordered society, and systems that invariably favour privilege and denigrate the poor and marginalized.

Many of us live in the hope, that perhaps, magical acts can bypass structures and thereby balance the books. In my experience, magic is invariably born from the contrasting, but necessary emotions of laughter and lament.

There are many definitions of magic, yet at the most elementary level, the nature of magic is expressed in two rhetorical questions.

*Do actions have consequences?*

*Can we change our actions, to change consequences?*

If you intuitively understand this, magic is straightforward.

Sigils for Magic is dedicated to the creative, artisan exploration of change and the action of change.

Jonathan Agento
July 2023

# 1

# LITTLE SQUIGGLES FOR SUCCESS

*"My mind jumbles things, reassembles them, and plays with words without even being asked." - Genesis P-Orridge*

We have all made sigils, well most of us anyway. Cast your mind back to when you were young, maybe in your early years of secondary school and you had a crush on someone. Sadly, as is often the case, they hadn't even noticed you. The first flush of unrequited love made you feel awkward, tongue tied and just a little anxious. Secretly you pictured a different scenario, where things were very different, one where your feelings were reciprocated. Perhaps you concluded that  it was just out of reach. Nevertheless, you would randomly doodle love hearts in your school exercise book entwined with their initials and yours. A seemingly unconscious act that expressed your intention as it flowed almost automatically onto the page. Well, that was a sigil.

I hope that it was successful, it probably helped, and it certainly increased the chances of you being noticed by the person concerned. Of course, their response may not have been the one you wanted.

A sigil is simply an intention in a condensed form. It contains information, contained in a unique format, that when activated, brings about a change in events. There are many ways to create sigils, they are as varied as language or art.

Sigil magic is probably the easiest form of magic available to anyone. It is not dependent upon any specific belief system, neither does it require a wealth of arcane knowledge, just a level of confidence and a little imagination. This introductory section gives some examples of simple instant sigils as a wry tribute to occultist Israel Regardie who defined a sigil as a 'signature'. It's a great analogy, as a signature both carries and conveys the presence and personality of the signatory. Here are some simple examples.

**Hurry up and serve me!**

Imagine you are waiting to be served at a bar, its busy and every time the barman comes near, he serves someone else. It takes all your patience to not shout out loud '*hurry up and serve me!*' Here is the monogram sigil you could draw in the spilt beer on the bar.

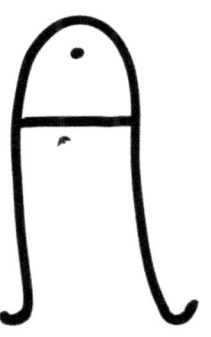

The intention 'hurry up' is abbreviated to an elongated U upturned with a line drawn across to form an H. The 'serve' is unnecessary, after all that is what barmen are paid to do. The 'me' is especially important and represented by a very definite dot made at the top of the image. The sigil points toward the barman who is being a bit of a 'dick' by not serving you. A sense of humour always seems to help with sigils.

It takes less than a second and requires 3 simple fluid movements. The sigil is simply activated by focussing your frustration into your intention as you draw it. If you are not convinced, try it out.

Another simple pictorial squiggle sigil can be used when a situation has reached an impasse. It could be that you are working on a project and a colleague is procrastinating and their indecision has caused everything to grind to a halt. Alternatively, it could apply to a relationship where you need to know where you stand.

## Shape up or ship out

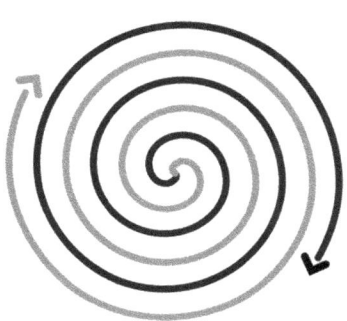

The first spiral depicts the chaos of indecision with an arrow towards one choice. A second spiral is drawn over, using a different colour, with an arrow pointing in the opposite direction. As with the previous example, the sigil is charged by your frustration at the chaos the indecision has caused. This sigil is particularly useful as it doesn't determine the particular outcome, it just forces a decision, so it is essential that you draw the arrows with complete indifference. Remember resolution is the only required outcome.

Another source of irritation, not dissimilar to waiting to be served at a bar, is being stuck at an event and ending up talking to someone you are seriously starting to detest. It may be that they possess zero sensory acuity and are unaware of your non-verbal feedback; or that they are simply monopolizing your company and preventing you from talking to someone else. Alternatively, it could be that they are always a 'pain in the ass' person and today is no exception. If you're not the sort of person who would tell them this to their face, there is a simple sigil you can use. It saves any unnecessary unpleasantness.

Not surprisingly, the intention is 'piss off' initialized, in this case the sigil isn't physically drawn, but conjured in the mind. It requires you to imagine the letters appearing in front of you, as if projected on a white board. Imagine the P with the o placed into space so it resembles a capital B. Next 'fold' this image diagonally along the middle, so the top of the P and the O line up.

As you do this, strongly recall the discomfort of having a very full bladder, and project this on the person you wish to be rid of. Hopefully there's a toilet nearby. Its particularly effective if you are directly opposite them. If you can recall the experience during later pregnancy of baby pushing down on your bladder, even better. I acknowledge that I can only attest to this second-hand.

I hope that by now you have recognised the simple action and dynamic humour required to create a simple sigil. At a basic level, a sigil is a shorthand intention that is activated by an obvious, 'pressing' need. It can be as simple and automatic as writing your own signature. The biggest problem at this stage is the apparent simplicity of the process. This of course, is its strength.

Sadly, we complicate things, when we were young, magic was a natural extension of an inquisitive imagination. Through play and storytelling, ordinary objects took on new identities as imagined beings interacted with us. Even when confronted with boredom, somehow our minds created 'playful' solutions.

At adolescence, a growing sense of self-awareness creates a challenging feedback loop, as our identities often adopt a series of personas to feel good about ourselves, or simply 'to fit in'. It's easy to dismiss these experiences as naïve, sometimes embarrassing experiments. Nevertheless, our childhood experiences showed us the possibility for change, many of these experiences defined who we are today.

Our development into adulthood sees an increasingly analytical mind attempting to resolve any new problems, often creating a series of potential scenarios, based upon experience or critical thinking. It's the most common form of problem solving, in these situations there is no need for magic, just logical thought, or good advice, maybe both. Job done.

However, there are always some scenarios where it seems impossible to know how to resolve a problem. In these situations, overthinking can be a curse. It may involve a personal need that we cannot share with a close friend, or when we need a solution immediately. Sometimes we can feel utterly powerless to change our circumstances and fulfil our dreams.

## So, what if things really were different?

In these situations, magic may hold some useful ideas and maybe the opportunity to engage ideas that stand just outside our experience. Magic is frequently described as *'the art or science of changing consciousness at will'* this often-cited definition seems a helpful place to start. Initially this seems to pose a problem highlighting a conflict with how we compartmentalise ideas.

Art is largely subjective, a matter of personal taste. Some art takes our breath away, as if the artist has completely captured our imagination, in contrast, other expressions leave us cold and unmoved. Science carries a sense of an objective quest, based upon standardised data, which whilst revealing variation, may be used to support a hypothesis. In many people's minds these disciplines exist poles apart, separated as 'soft' art and 'hard' science. Regardless of where you personally stand on this, we can conclude they are both very necessary human activities. Art and science represent some of our greatest aspirations and achievements as a species.

Magic, provided it isn't too tightly defined, shares much in common with art and science. All three are concerned with results as an expression of intention. Magic is an artisan craft, uniquely curated by the will, preferences, and desires of the magician, mixed with the persistence and curiosity of scientific enquiry.

Results really do matter, how they are achieved, is a matter of personal taste.

Having briefly considered the relationship between art, science and magic, the final part of our working definition of magic requires the ability to 'change consciousness at will'.

Human consciousness is a complex topic. Is life an external experience we observe by looking outwards, or an internal projection of our own making?

I'm not proposing there is a direct answer to this question, perhaps it is a mixture of both, simply that it is possible to transform how we experience a situation, by changing consciousness and adopting a different perspective. Sigil magic uses several techniques, sometimes called 'gnosis' to achieve an altered state of consciousness. So far, we have considered straightforward examples of frustration and the memory of an urgent physical experience. There are many ways to change consciousness.

The role of the will is central to magic. It can be as simple as getting your own way in a situation. This can create problems if you believe you are not entitled to have your own way, or if you lack sufficient empathy to recognise a need for compromise for a situation to change. An excess of entitlement is an unpleasant trait, one guaranteed to ensure obstacles block your path. Too much empathy for others, without consideration for yourself, could turn you into a doormat. Aligning your will alongside an attitude of empathy for others seems a good place to start.

Successful sigil magic does raise other questions; 'did I get what I wanted?' 'Did it happen as expected?' and 'do I still want it now that I have it?' These are questions about our own reflexivity and self-reflection.

It may be that 'our will' is considerably more complex that simply our immediate desires. The examination of these ideas, combined with a little creative flair and a sense of humour, provides the basis for successful sigil magic.

However, to be able to access these ideas and questions, you will have to be able to silence the internal monologue that runs continuously through your head. Not all trains of thought are helpful, some simply reflect unhelpful cultural conditioning, others just 'bog you down'.

## Clearing your head

For these and other reasons, most magical practitioners use a form of grounding activity as a prelude to working magic and can create a light trance state in which you may become more conscious, or less conscious of your thoughts, physical sensations, and emotions.

## Technique 1

*Pranyama* or 'breath control' is a simple yoga technique that regulates breathing to calm the mind. This example is sometimes called 'square breathing' and its aim is to slightly elongate your normal breathing, through four conscious steps, whilst counting to four. You can use this pretty much anywhere, although it is more effective if you can lie flat or sit with your back straight.

1. **Inhale** – count to four.
2. **Pause** - count to four.
3. **Exhale** - count to four.
4. **Pause** - count to four.

Repeat this several times, so that each step flows in even cycles that are more consistent and slightly longer than your normal breathing.

Many people find it difficult to sit and do nothing. Sit still and notice just how many thoughts randomly pop into your head.

Once you have achieved this you may experience physical impulses to move, twitch or scratch. These can be challenging to resist.

Most of the time we do not even notice that we are constantly reacting to impulses and habits in our minds and bodies. If you can turn these down for a short period, then you are developing some useful skills by allowing space for your mind and body to relax. If your head is constantly battered by human folly, hyper partisan media threads and despair at the destruction of the environment, it's a great place to reset.

## Technique 2

This is best performed sitting relaxed and upright, if you lie down, you may fall asleep. Ensure you will not be disturbed and set a gentle alarm to alert you in twenty minutes.

When you are comfortable notice your breathing, close your eyes and count each inhale and exhale as one cycle. Repeat this process ten times. Continue counting to ten until you are aware of your alarm reminding you that twenty minutes have elapsed.

Initially, this can seem frustrating, random thoughts will pop into your head to distract you from the process. You can acknowledge these thoughts as they arise and simply let them go by not dwelling on them. If you like you can imagine counting your breathing as a train running smoothly along the tracks, each interruption of thought, is simply *a station that the train is not stopping at*.

All these are strategies for you to regain control of your body, it's surprising how many thoughts and sensations press in upon us. If you have found these particularly challenging there are plenty of video clips to help, most towns have classes offering similar techniques.

American writer, magician and visual artist, William S. Burroughs developed *The Doing Easy* (1973) as a process for mastering tasks, it has been a popular preparation technique for magicians ever since. Burroughs uses the example of tidying a room, often an irritating chore.

> '*You can start right now tidying up your flat, moving furniture or books, washing dishes, making tea, sorting papers. Consider the weight of objects exactly how much force is needed to get the object from here to there. Consider its shape and texture and function where exactly does it belong. Use just the amount of force necessary to get the object from here to there. When you touch an object weigh it with your fingers, feel your fingers on the object, the skin, blood, muscles, tendons of you hand and arm. Never let a poorly executed sequence pass. If you throw a match at a wastebasket and miss; repeat the sequence until objects are brought to order. Once you find the easy way you do not have to think about it. You can land objects in that wastebasket over your shoulder. You know how to touch and move and pick up things. Objects move into place at your lightest touch. You slip into actions, like a film, moving with such ease you hardly know you are doing it'.*

The more skilful you become at accomplishing a task, the less work your brain as to do. It becomes almost automatic to the extent you don't need to think about your actions. This has an obvious advantage in casting sigils, where temporary focus on a symbolic representation needs to be released and forgotten quickly.

# 2

# MONOGRAMS OF THOUGHT

*"Embrace reality by imagination" - OM Spare*

The act of encapsulating an intention in an image is as old as humanity itself. Our earliest ancestors dreamed of hunting, perhaps, the prime reason for such beautiful examples of Palaeolithic cave art. Recently, many examples of this artform have been re-examined by Canadian anthropologist Genevieve von Petzinger. In *The First Signs* (2016) she reveals a series of symbols - spirals, crosses, dots, triangles, and parallel lines, that appear towards the edge of these pictures. For thousands of years these remained unnoticed, obscured by the predominant artwork. Remarkably the same 32 designs have been found in caves thousands of miles apart, spanning a period of 20,000 years. Long before the birth of any common language, universal symbols were conveying information. Their ability to codify and transmit graphic messages beyond a single moment in time is hugely significant in our evolution as a species. It's hard to imagine the reassuring impact of these messages on pioneering travellers entering unknown and potentially dangerous landscapes. Our earliest ancestor's survival and wellbeing may well have depended on such sigils. I suspect there will be many discoveries following Petzinger's research.

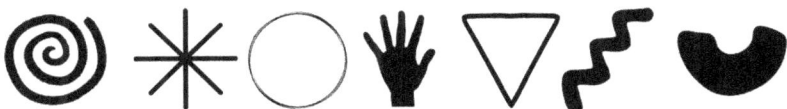

**Some of the signs discovered by Genevieve von Petzinger**

Pictorial Writing or hieroglyphic symbols are commonly associated with the artistic traditions of Egypt 4000 BCE onwards. They may represent objects they depict, or particular sounds or groups of sounds. All these ideas are significant in sigil magic. Interestingly the word hieroglyph (sacred carving) is a Greek translation of the Egyptian phrase 'god's words' and indicates a system older than handwritten cursive script. Similar graphic transitions occurred in different parts of the world.

The Latin alphabet, which is in common usage in the Western World, was originally based upon the Greek alphabet and introduced throughout the Roman empire. After the fall of this empire, it was standardized by Charlemagne in 800CE, which heralded the emergence of the Middle Ages. Originally the preserve of an educated religious elite, written language provided the transition into the modern world.

Despite the wealth of written words, pictorial images have continued to flourish, from medieval Coats of Arms, to late twentieth century corporate logos and branding and twenty-first century memes and emoji. Ask any advertising company, the right logo says everything without saying a word. Sigils are everywhere.

## The Transformation of Sigils

Religion and magic have always co-habited, with some religions developing complex magical rituals. This makes it difficult to entirely separate the two. The amalgamation or syncretism of religious beliefs ensured traditional or folk magic have remained protected under a religious veneer. History is not a singular storyline, relayed unbroken through a chain of command. It fluctuates, flourishes, falls, and rises within a changing cultural context.

The overlap of religion, science, and art during the Renaissance contributed to the growth of differing schools of magical

thought, collectively known as the Western Magical Tradition. These schools gained popularity in the late 19th century and drew upon themes within Greek and Egyptian mystery traditions, including Gnosticism, Neoplatonism, Hermeticism and a metaphysical reading of the Bible. Astrology, Alchemy, and divination provided insights into the upward journey of the soul. In many respects its appeal was to the past and the rediscovery of magical textbooks or grimoires. Magicians painstakingly replicated complex symbols, seals, and sigils to evoke spirits, summon demons, charge talismans to gain insights, and achieve mastery over destiny.

This tradition would have continued unchallenged were it not for avant-garde artist and magician Austin Osman Spare (1886 – 1956) who played a central role in reframing modern sigil magic. Spare adopts a straightforward approach and makes sigils accessible to those outside of ceremonial magical societies. An analogy with language is helpful here, where for example, correct spelling and grammar is considered a hallmark of good education. Within traditional occult thought, a misplaced mark or glyph could render a magical working invalid. Spare concluded that there are no correct or incorrect sigils. Perfect spelling and grammatical-grimoire-perfection are therefore irrelevant. Spare skilfully moves sigil magic from the past into the present. In many ways he anticipated the anarchic, non-conformist attitude of later youth culture. Twenty years after his death, his ideas provided the inspiration for Chaos Magick, which has continuously developed sigil casting. Whilst Spare might not have endorsed all the subsequent revisions of sigil magic, he is responsible for the 'pandorian unboxing' of sigil magic that was to influence (among others) the Illuminates of Thanateros and the post-punk magical collective Thee Temple ov Psychic Youth.

The value of the sigil lies in the simple acknowledgement that it is uniquely created by the magician. This may (or may not) reference historic or contemporary aspects of art, science, and religion. There is something remarkably refreshing and effective about creating artisan magic.

It is also worth considering the impact of the French occultist, Alphonse Louis Constant (1810 – 1875), better known as Eliphas Lévi, who would greatly influence magic and modern witchcraft. His views can be simplified into three principles.

1) The role of will is the real force behind magic, consequently all magical and ritual paraphernalia are simply 'props' to aid the will. 2) An underlying 'light', not unlike Ether, permeates and connects all realms. 3) There is a direct, causal relationship between microcosm and macrocosm and a corresponding role of 'like attracting like' across seen and unseen realms. These ideas can be understood and utilized the magician.

> *"To attain the sanctum regnum, in other words, the knowledge and power of the Magi, there are four indispensable conditions; an intelligence illuminated by study, an intrepidity which nothing can check, a will which cannot be broken, and a prudence which nothing can corrupt, and nothing intoxicate".*

Thankfully Levi simplifies this into a formula:

*"To know, to will, to dare, to keep silence."*

He concludes:

> *"These are the four words of the Magus (Magician), inscribed upon the four symbolical forms of the sphinx."*
>
> Transcendental Magic (1854 & 1856).

The Sphinx was often depicted as a mythical creature with head of a human, body of a lion, & wings of an eagle, it's function was to guard the mysteries, and erected outside temples to provide protection.

Levi's formula was described by Paul Huson in *Mastering Witchcraft* (1970) as *'a virulent imagination, a will of fire, a rock-hard faith, and a flair for secrecy'*. I first came across these ideas in my youth as the Powers of the Sphinx and rediscovered them in my training in witchcraft as taught by my mentor and friend, High Priestess, and Craft Elder, Maureen Wheeler, as the Witches Pyramid.

## The Witches Pyramid and Sigil Magic

A little scaffolding can help with sigil magic. The witches pyramid can work as a standalone practice, it is not necessary to have any specific beliefs, or identify as a witch. You can employ any beliefs you may have; you can also exchange these for other beliefs, as appropriate. The point is not really to believe in anything, the goal is to create sigils and observe how they work.

**To know** – A clear intention, ensure you know exactly what you want and why you want it.

**To will** – The process of condensing or encoding your intention into a sigil.

**To dare** – The act of charging your sigil with energy.

**To keep silent** - Releasing and forgetting your sigil.

In summary, sigils require knowledge, intentional will, daring in their release combined with silent peace to 'seal' them.

Follow these four principles and sigil magic is straightforward.

# The Reverse Countdown Method

In previous examples, initial letters were used as a form of abbreviated intention drawn or imagined 'as a flowing monogram of thought'. One of the most common methods for creating a sigil was introduced by Spare and developed by others. It entails removing either vowels, repeat letters or both. This is simply a method to reduce the statement to make it easier to work with and shift your comprehension from the conscious to the unconscious mind.

I call it the 'reverse countdown method' and (unlike Spare) use both uppercase and lowercase letters as it creates more opportunities to 'morph' letters into shapes. It is my favourite method of sigil design.

The first task is deciding exactly what you intend to happen. Your initial statement should focus on the outcome. It should be short, simple, and direct.

General principles to ensure you get what you want.

- Use positive words rather than negative words.
- Have fixed or clear goals - you can include a timeline.
- Use the present tense.
- Focus on the 'finished' outcome rather than describing the desire to get there.

Having spent many years teaching in secondary schools, the instruction 'don't forget your homework' produces a low result, whereas 'bring me your completed homework next lesson' is a clearer and more successful direction. Homework sucks.

Here are two examples.

**Example 1**: Intentional statement - *I will have a new flat.*

First, remove the vowels, so 10 consonants remain.

Second, remove the repeating letters, seven consonants remain (See figure 1).

Third, create sigil from remaining consonants. You can overlay similar shapes (See figure 2).

I will have a new flat
   w ll h vn       w fl t
   w l h vn         f t
   w l h v n f t

Figure 1

Figure 2

In figure 2, I have used an upper-case H within the f, creating a T masking the l. The v is hidden in the W, the N is located within the W. This is the strength of using both upper and lower-case letters in your sigil design.

**Example 2**: Intentional statement - *I will pass my exams.*

Remove vowels & repeat letters.

     w l p s my x

     merge w & m

     Place x & y together

Turn S into infinity symbol, this is always an interesting symbol (which conveys its own sense of perpetual motion) to include, particularly if the sigil needs to work for the duration of all your exams.

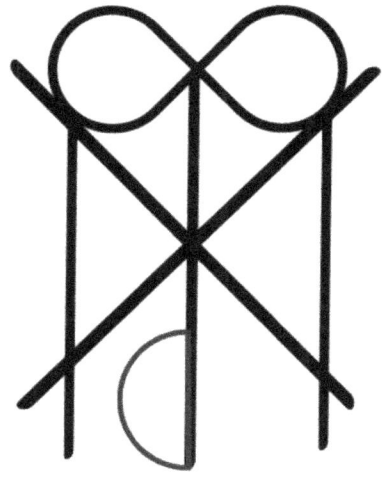

No two sigils are ever likely to look the same, these are simply my examples. There are no rules as to how your sigil should look, so long as it works for you.

Spend time playing with letters and their shapes it will help your sigil construction.

## Releasing a Sigil

This is one simple, but highly effective, method for creating, charging it with intention and releasing a sigil by thrusting it into the back of your subconscious.

Write your completed sigil on a piece of paper. You will need a candle and a flameproof bowl or cauldron where you can safely drop your burning sigil. Spend a few minutes in silent meditation and prepare yourself.

When you are ready, light the candle and pick up your sigil.

Stare intently at your sigil, your original intent is irrelevant at this stage, only the sigil is significant. Take a deep breath and drink in the image, noticing its form and shape.

As you breathe out, infuse the sigil with your energy.

Repeat this process of breathing in and breathing out a few times, until the image of your sigil becomes your only thought. You can increase the rate of your breathing to better charge your sigil.

Hold up the sigil so the edge of the paper just touches the flame and allow it to burn, until the flames reach your fingers. The approaching heat warning of impending pain will break your focus, quickly drop the burning sigil into the dish. Your sigil is released.

Carefully extinguish any flames, including the candle and forget your intention and your sigil. Do something completely different that will keep you completely distracted from your intention. Think of it no more.

Strangely, the hardest part of mastering these techniques is the final act of forgetting. If you are old enough to remember watching *Fawlty Towers* you may well recall John Cleese trying not to 'mention the war' becoming an embarrassingly repetitive storyline. Remembering something funny and laughing out loud is an effective technique to change your physiology and conclude sigil magic.

If you have really been paying attention, you may have noticed a potential conflict in the two earlier examples in this chapter. These concern the use of the future and present phrasing of your intentional statements. For example, 'I will have a new flat' could imply an event in the future, rather than an immanent one.

You could change your statement to 'I have a new flat' which brings it into the present. However, this may cause a conflict, on one hand this is what you want, but maybe you don't have it yet. The oscillation between these may well negatively influence the outcome of your sigil. One way to resolve this is to always focus upon the 'will' aspect as an expression of intent.

Some of these dilemmas vanish when the sigil is reduced down to letters rather than words. With a little practice you will find the most effective way to express your intention.

You may wish to keep a record of your sigils in a journal. This is helpful in building your confidence in their success. Make a copy your sigil before you charge it and record your original intention with date and timeframe on a different page in your journal. It is important to keep the actual sigil and its intention separately once it has been cast. You created your sigil with a specific goal in mind and intentionally chose to forget it, now only your unconscious is aware of the sigil.

# 3
# SEASHORE SIGILS

*"The sea, once it casts its spell, holds one in the net of wonder forever"* - Jacques Cousteau

Some locations lend themselves to magic. We all have places that we consider magical, here - it is easy to trip the switch of our consciousness and set change in motion. A favourite place of mine is a hidden beach reached by crossing mud flats by an almost abandoned Saxon church. The liminal space where the land, sky and sea meet are an ideal place to launch sigils.

You can charge and release a simple sigil on a sunny day at the beach. Spend a few moments observing the sunlight glistening on the surface of the water. Slowly narrow your view by slightly bringing together your eyelids, so that your only focus is the glinting light on the glossy water. If it is not a sunny day, you can use the regular sound and motion of waves, it will have the same effect. After a couple of minutes this should induce a light trance and shift your consciousness, from this point of gnosis, you can draw your sigil in the sand. With a little practice beforehand, you should be able to do this as a continuous, barely conscious, action. If you are on a deserted beach with an incoming tide, you can allow the waves to wash your sigil away. Alternatively wipe the sigil out with your eyes closed.

A seashore location for sigil magic is particularly helpful to understand the pattern and process of sigil casting. Every sigil makes a journey from intention to symbol, only to be flipped back into your subconscious and then out, or deeper in, to exert influence and bring change. Seas and oceans are great examples of this, vast bodies of water that ebb and flow, always changing, always in motion. This change is manifest through the tides. There are two high tides and two low tides in a period of 24 hours and 50 minutes. You can utilize tidal energy to cast your sigil. As we live on an island, most historic changes have occurred through contact via the sea with other cultures and ideas. The sea is the portal, the point of connection for change. Use a receding, ebb tide for getting rid of or banishing something and an incoming, flow or flood tide to draw something to you or for growth and expansion.

One of my favourite moments is the point at which the tide is about to turn. This is a great time to consider choices, perhaps whether you should proceed or turn back in a particular course of action.

The ever-changing seashore provides its own inspiration for creating sigils, pretty much everything you need is there carried by the sea, all you need is a sharpie pen.

You could draw your sigil on a flat stone and skim it across the water like a bouncing bomb to release its intention. You can place a series of these on top of a wooden groyne to link multiple sigils and allow the incoming tide to wash them away.

Alternatively, you could place a sigil on a piece of paper inside a clam shell and bind it shut with twine, sea grass or seaweed. You can use discarded fishing net to bind or entangle something you wish to be free from; or to catch or ensnare something you desire. However, don't return any nylon net to the sea, simply dispose of it appropriately. To birth a project, you can place your sigil within the tough, leathery egg cases known as devil's purses or mermaid's purses. Once your sigil is tightly bound - cast it into the sea to release it.

Another coastal technique for sigil magic uses hag stones, these are sometimes called holey stones or adder stones. They are often found at beaches and sometimes in rivers, where the continual pounding pressure of water or other objects wears a hole through the stone. There are many uses for hag stones, the most common are for protection, against illness, nightmares, and evil spirits. They are ideal places to put a rolled-up healing or protection sigil, which can be cast into the sea or hung on a red cord. In a similar way hag stones are also believed to promote fertility, so a suitable sigil could be placed in the hag stone and worn or hung up in a bedroom.

Another feature of hag stones is their ability to act as portals to another realm and they can be used in conjunction with a suitable sigil, for scrying, seeing future events and journeying to the underworld.

Tidal currents and waves create their own magic. Narrow spits of shingle enable walking right out into the sea without getting too wet and providing you have checked the tides, returning safely. Here the element of fear provides the means to release your sigil. These spits also create their own criss-crossing waves, great for sowing discord and mayhem. One West Country witch had to call emergency services, when one member of their group got caught out by a strong current. Always exercise caution when using tidal energies, particularly during spring tides and stormy weather.

The following account is taken from my journal and describes a journey progressing towards the release of two sigils at the seashore.

### Full Moon November

> *Driving through the darkness, along a peninsula once cut off by the sea. Past the old ferry station -journeying along land now reclaimed, that inevitably will be returned to the water. Twisting lanes narrowing, hedges reflecting dipped headlights, dance like waves around me.*
>
> *Solitary passing spaces in the lane, remind me of my own necessary seclusion. Slowing down to avoid potholes until*

*I can park somewhere safely hidden and out of sight. Stepping out, walking carefully, quietly, opening the wooden gate, knowing that with the click of the heavy latch - my presence will not be disturbed.*

*Emerging from the darkness is a small building, one remaining chancel, remnant of a Saxon Church one of the first in Sussex, now seldom used. Guarded by dark headstones, remnants of the loved, the lost and the lonely.*

*Bowing to history and mindful of magic to follow, with a wry smile, I pay my respects. Beginning my slow, sinstral walk around the church completing, seven widdershin circuits, in silent meditation.*

*Pausing to invite those among the dead who wish to join my journey and aid my magic, I move steadily onwards, opening the gate and leaving the churchyard. Turning to my left, walking softly past a long-gone Castle, its remaining mound and water-filled moat resembles a smaller Silbury hill. I smile as I remember past rituals held there.*

*The path leads down to the earie mud flats - flooded and sometimes impassable at high tide, the stillness broken by owls in the distance, curlews in the wetlands - concerned by my presence and maybe by those accompanying me.*

*Occasionally the hint of the full moon illuminates the ghostly, liminal, watery marshlands - only to vanish behind clouds.*

*The sea remains unseen beyond, tucked behind the banked-up shingle. I can hear it though, hidden waves crashing - this sends shivers down my spine or am I just cold or just slightly afraid?*

*Walking becomes harder now and the climb up the shifting stones requires my full attention. Finally, in front of me lies the sea, a vast liminal portal between the realms - the tide about halfway to full - with a small patch of sand to my left.*

*Walking to the water's edge I make offerings and perform a simple ritual. The moon fully appears, hanging beacon like in the night sky - illuminating miles of empty beach, moonlight flickering trance-like on glossy water.*

*Taking a piece of folded paper, I pause, then shout my petition, waiting...... for the right moment when a wave slaps my legs, the cold water makes me laugh as I hurl my sigil into the water.*

*After a few moments I turn away and return to the solitary strip of sand to draw a healing sigil for a friend's mother. Using driftwood and shells I build a little altar over it for her recovery.*

*Feelings of joy and gratitude arise, the moon has energized the night-sky reflecting perfectly in the water 'as above so below'. The incoming tide will cover and return all things. I have done what I can, what I must.*

*After about 15 minutes I feel cold and drawing everything together, retrace my steps along the mud flats, with the sound of geese flying over me.*

*'Gathering all magic in' – I walk back, returning the departed to the churchyard, carefully and purposefully shutting the gate and return to my car.*

The occultist, Dion Fortune, in *The Sea Priestess* (1938) perfectly describes the relationship between the energy of the sea with magic.

> "I saw the sea-gods come, moving with an irresistible momentum, not rising into the air as the riders rose, but deep in their own element, unhasting, unresting; for the power of the sea is in the weight of the waters and not in the wind-blown crests. These Great Ones rose with the tide, and like the tide, nothing might withstand them."

## Lammas 2022

This ritual was based upon the above text and loosely on the seashore ritual found in Janet and Stuart Farrar's *A Witches' Bible* (1981). It was performed as a group activity in the evening at a secluded beach. During the ritual a woman emerges from the water representing the goddess Isis, raising her arms in a curve and makes the following declaration.

> *I am the soundless, boundless, dark sea.*
> *All tides are mine, and answer to me.*
> *The tides turn at Lammas, all is cut back!*
> *Tides of the airs, tides of the inner earth,*
> *the secret tides of death and birth.*
> *The tides of souls, dreams, and destiny.*
> *I come to those who call to me and seek liberty.*

The fire of Azrael is lit, burning juniper, cedar, and sandalwood. All inhale the smoke and trance oracles are given.

Sigils are inscribed on stones and cast into the sea. As a final act of release, we all run into the sea. The cool water breaks any focus on the sigil, laughter, splashing, and merriment follow. Above us an orange moon reflects on the breaking waves, turning the wind-blown crests the colour of gold. It was a beautifully simple and highly memorable ritual, combining traditional occult practice with modern sigil casting, followed by a magical, moonlight swim.

Sigils can be cast anywhere. Sometimes it's worth finding a location where the atmosphere and setting provide the right context.

Magic is a state of mind, an openness to experiencing and influencing change. It involves a range of emotions and events that overlap each other with an uncanny synchronicity. Whilst sitting quietly on the same beach I felt trance like words coming to me, possibly a delayed reaction to inhaling the smoke from the fire of Azrael. Thankfully I always carry my phone so they could be typed into its notebook.

*Whispers on the winds, witches who 'whistle the winds', know these things.*

*The inevitable outcome of fire meets ice.*

*The sea that rises, is not thriving, but dying. Carrying the dead of millennia – acidic, toxic, it has nowhere to go, other than to recover the earth.*

*The land knows this, torrents of saline pain, carried on the winds, whispering 'we are coming', powerless to halt. The earth spirits fear the salt.*

*The land rendered barren, bleached. Animals sense this, beached and corralled, habitats cramped like holidaymakers at high tide, vying for space.*

*In the future we are all refugees.*

Magic is invariably born from observation and intuition. A mind that is alert, listening to landscapes, mindful of events that are unfolding, can consider alternative scenarios. Here we can find hope.

The super-rich may be able to avoid the events that threaten to engulf us all, by moving to the safety of heavily guarded hideaways high above the rising sea levels and bush fires or plan an escape for a select existence on another planet. Whilst the rest of us are left wondering how we ever ended up devouring a planet, in pursuit of 'things' we were told would make our lives better.

Sigil magic may well be the best solution to everyday issues and needs, but I sincerely hope it also provides some answers to bigger issues, as Rhyd Wildermuth notes in *The Secret of Crossings* (2022):

> *"We can only hope perhaps there are still some secret paths that can be forded. Maybe not for all of humanity, nor even for most of us, but maybe at least the few who still look for those crossings: those who stand in awe at the larger forces of nature our false god 'Progress' has unleashed."*

# 4
# SONOROUS SORCERY

*"Sigils are, by their nature, ascetically vocal"* - JA

Ask any communicator - words matter, not just the actual vocabulary, but how they sound. Some phonic sounds have universal impact. The word *Ameen*, also pronounced *ahmen, aymen, amen* or *amin*, is used in Judaism, Christianity, and Islam to express agreement and often translated *"so be it"*. It is believed to have originated from an ancient Semitic word consisting of three letters: A-M-N. This is not dissimilar to the Sanskrit A-U-M, chanted in Indian philosophy as '*the creative sound that brings all things into manifestation*'. Sounds are evocative.

Many linguists have suggested that the word sigil is probably based upon the Latin *sigilum* meaning sign; but also, that it may be derived from the Hebrew word *segula* which can mean '*a charm that supersedes logic*'. This is quite a good definition of magic. Sometimes segula can be translated as 'word-action'. This seems very apt. A sigil can also be a spoken word or specific sound.

A hieroglyphic can be a sigil. This Greek word comprises of two words 'holy' and 'symbol'. It can be understood in two ways; a sacred carved symbol or a holy or 'distinctly separate' word-symbol. In its holy sense devout Jews avoid using g-ds name outside of a devotional setting, as it is considered too sacred to be uttered in everyday life. It is certainly a powerful word, reciting it was strong enough magic, for Adam's first wife Lilith, to freely leave the heavily guarded garden of Eden. In this respect it became a spoken sigil of self-determinism.

If these examples are too monotheist for your taste, I recently observed an open ritual at a pagan camp where the priestess publicly used secret god/dess names in the opening invocation. The look on some faces, including a visiting American professor who was a Wiccan, was priceless. Some words are for select audiences. Some words are spoken sigils.

Bizarrely (or not) as a young man I worked with exorcists in rural Zambia. It was a life changing experience, I witnessed unimaginable poverty, infectious joy and traditional superstitions, falling asleep each night to the sound of distant drums. In the local Lamba dialect, the word used to cast out spirits was *'koya.'* However, it was not working very well. Unsettling commotions and bizarre behaviour at public gatherings were causing panic in many communities and disrupting village life. Enter a visiting linguistics expert who reminded them of an obscure local word, only used to describe the act of 'kicking a dog out of the way' and before you could say 'hey presto' the exorcists were back in business. Specific words are especially useful in magic by virtue of the image and energy they generate in our unconscious mind. Naturally, this example is not meant to endorse cruelty towards animals. I love dogs.

Maybe it is the value of an unfamiliar language, but many years later I was struck by the French word *tombe* which means 'all fall down' (incidentally I always thought it was etombe). It finds expression in the English word entombed. Sometime later at a pagan camp in the New Forest I was asked to chaperone a friend's daughter, who was recovering from a serious illness, it was no hardship, she was good company and a pretty girl. For this reason, she attracted quite a lot of unwanted attention, particularly from one person, who was creeping her out. One evening whilst sitting around the main fire pit, he overstepped the mark again, and she asked me to intervene. Whilst he was heading towards her, I threw the word tombe at him, his legs gave way and he collapsed, falling perilously close to the fire pit, much to everyone's amusement. He did not bother her again.

Several years later I discovered that a friend, who suffered from depression and lived some distance away, had taken a potentially fatal overdose. I called another friend, local to her, and he had an ambulance sent to her house. The paramedics arrived and told me that she would not let them in and the only reason they would break in, would be if they saw her collapse. We both remotely projected tombe at her, thankfully she collapsed by a window in full view of a paramedic, and the crew were able to break the door down, take her to hospital where her stomach was pumped, and she made a full recovery. Today she is a remarkably astute therapist and healer.

Some words seem to convey their meaning well, simply through sound. To add visual strength, you can link the word-sound to a visual image.

The Tower card in the major arcana tarot deck captures the energy of tombe. It can be helpful to have a mental image of your word and incorporate into your sigil.

Below is my contribution to the international 'Hex Him' sigil campaign, using the phrase 'Tombe Trump' including the trump card the Tower XVI.

Words and their predecessors, hieroglyphics, all convey meaning, feelings, and aspirations. They are shapes that we read, or perhaps more accurately recognise, and understood – they speak to us.

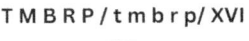

You can use pretty much any word as a sigil, it just needs to encapsulate a unique meaning to you.

You could create a word to chant using the vowel and repeat letter removal method - however this is more challenging as there less than a dozen words in the English language with no vowels. It is difficult to chant a mantra with no vowels. There is nothing to suggest sigils are necessarily inhibited by vowels! For example, you could compress your intention and then add in a couple of vowels to assist its tonal sound.

Intention - *I have good judgement.*

Remove vowels and repeat letters so it becomes *hvgdjmnt*, rearrange and add in a few random vowels and you get this:

*jahv minit god?*

Try chanting that for a while, and your judgement will improve. Laughter is great magic.

If that seems too complicated, just play with words. Sometimes they will just come together almost by their own will. Whilst working on an anti-fracking sigil, the phrase 'Cuadrilla Driller-Killer' popped into my head, perfectly encapsulating both the intention, and creating an image of a blood-spattered maniac with a power tool to take down that company. Its rolls off the tongue nicely, chants well, and is a rather good example of sonorous sorcery.

There are plenty of untapped techniques such as varieties of shorthand which work with the phonetics of words. If you have had to learn shorthand or any system of annotation use it to your advantage in sigil construction.

A simple written technique which can be chanted or written involves writing down someone's name and then writing your intention over their name. The number three is considered powerful in most magical traditions, so three squared is particularly potent. In Hoodoo, a magical tradition developed by enslaved Africans in the Southern States of America, where this technique probably originates, the number nine is used for endings, curses, and diminishment. The name and intended recipient of your sigil are written nine times. There are many variations on this theme.

Image you are being hassled by someone. Your intention might be 'piss off, leave me alone.' This reduces rather nicely to *polma* which would make a great sigil to chant to mutter or under your breath.

Even better if you know their name. They could be a work colleague, an ex-partner, or a particularly persistent salesperson. Or perhaps an arrogant evangelist, or as I call them 'ego'gelists, as they believe their view is always unequivocally right.

This example uses the name Steve (my apologies to anyone with this name).

Write 'Steve' out nine times and overlay (in red, perhaps) your monogrammed intention *'polma'*:

Steve    Steve    Steve
Steve    Steve    Steve
Steve    Steve    Steve

You could fold up the paper, folding away from you, as your intention is for Steve to leave you alone. You could intone polma whilst your burn your sigil.

Alternatively, you quite fancy Charly, but are unsure if they will agree to a date, you could use this:

*Come On A Date With Me (coadwm)*

Charly  Charly  Charly

Charly  Charly  Charly

Charly  Charly  Charly

In this instance you would fold the paper towards you. Whilst deliberately manipulating someone else might be morally questionable, this sigil allows you to spend some time with the person and perhaps impress them. Magic increases the likelihood of events occurring.

To charge your intentional sigil, you could burn as in the previous example. An excellent hoodoo technique is to place your folded paper in your waistband, so the friction of movement and your sweat wears the sigil out. Alternatively, you could place it under the insole of your shoe, to the same effect.

This is a version I have used with hundreds of people a few years ago. I was particularly impressed by one person who released and shredded their sigil by placing it under their car and wheel spinning over it. I used my version at the coast under a full moon.

Sigils do work and Trump was impeached within next lunar cycle. He eventually managed to evade this charge twice, so the working was only partially successful. The deflection of this charge may be due to the influence of Christian fundamentalist intercessors and 'prayer warriors' charged with creating a protective POTUS shield over the President of the United States.

I sincerely hope he gets what he is due. His recent indictment is a step in the right direction.

# 5
# Dot-to-dot Sudoku

*"Everything's intentional. It's just filling in the dots"*
*- David Byrne*

If like me, you are not a great artist, unable able to style an appealing sigil with a few deft swishes, how about if you had a grid where you simply joined the dots? That's a *kamea*.

If some sigils are a variation on a reverse Countdown, magic squares or kameas are more like dot-to-dot Sudoku. The number square provides both the parameter and vectors for the construction of a sigil. A kamea is a representation of dynamic planetary forces in a mathematical format.

The earliest known magic square, the Chinese Lo Shu, dates from the 1st century. By the end of the first millennium, magic squares had travelled through India, into Arabia and were recorded in the encyclopaedic Rasa'il. For the last two thousand years magicians have been using these types of sigils to gain self-knowledge and influence events. In a ritual magic, this is a complex process, requiring a knowledge of the Kabbala, planetary magic and often the Hebrew language. Thankfully, not all magic needs to be complicated and many of these ideas can be used, without having to roll up a trouser leg or make a blood oath, simply to join an arcane secret society.

To create a sigil using a kamea all the usual principles apply, but rather than condensing words, the letters are given a number value. When these are placed in the appropriate planetary grid the sigil is created. The advantage of this process is that the attributes of a particular planet influence both the creation and action of a sigil.

Perhaps the easiest way to create a sigil using a Kamea would use a keyword that best describes your intention. In this example is it to become a more proficient magician.

The Lo Shu kamea, often called the square of Saturn, is used to gain discipline to complete a goal, so rather appropriate for the sigil. It is also the simplest example to demonstrate the process.

**Square of Saturn**

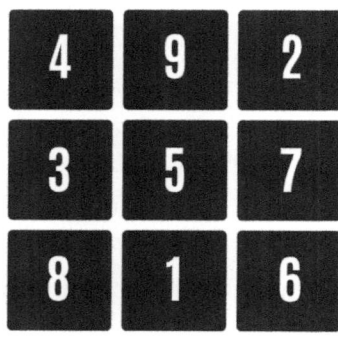

This kamea comprises of three key numbers. The first one is the planetary number 3, the second is the square of the planetary number which equals 9. The third is the sum of the numbers used (1-9) which equals 45 divided by the planetary number (3) which then equals 15. All the columns, rows and diagonals add up to 15.

Using the Pythagorean numerology table, letters have a numerological value.

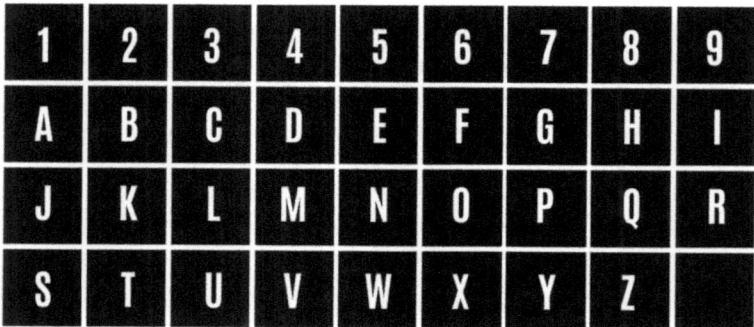

The keyword **Magician** is converted to numbers:

| m | a | g | i | c | i | a | n |
|---|---|---|---|---|---|---|---|
| 4 | 1 | 7 | 9 | 3 | 9 | 1 | 5 |

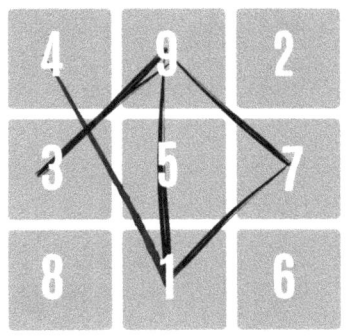

The sigil is drawn by plotting the path of 'magician' in the Square of Saturn kamea.

Draw a line from the 4 to 1, then from 1 to 7, then 7 to 9 and continue this until you have used all eight numbers.

Remove the shape from the box.

You might notice that your shape resembles something like a fish or a kite. If this is a strong image in your mind, you might want to just use that (or indeed any variation of that shape) as your pictorial sigil.

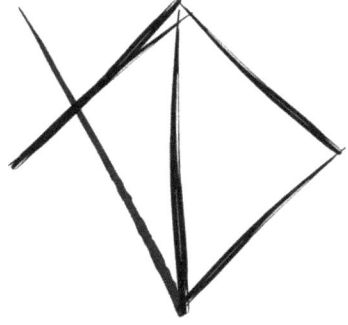

You could also play with the shape until you are happy with your finished sigil.

All planetary Kamea's have a representation as specific sigil that acts as a seal. You will notice the following planetary squares contain a wide range of numbers. Jupiter influences success, abundance, money, growth and activities involving chance whereas Mars influences confidence, assertion, sexuality, energy and strength (including competitive sports).

## Square of Jupiter

| 4  | 14 | 15 | 1  |
|----|----|----|----|
| 9  | 7  | 6  | 12 |
| 5  | 11 | 10 | 8  |
| 16 | 2  | 3  | 13 |

## Square of Mars

| 11 | 24 | 7  | 20 | 3  |
|----|----|----|----|----|
| 4  | 12 | 25 | 8  | 16 |
| 17 | 5  | 13 | 21 | 9  |
| 10 | 18 | 1  | 14 | 22 |
| 23 | 6  | 19 | 2  | 15 |

Unless you have studied planetary magic in detail, you can simply use the existing seal as a sigil.

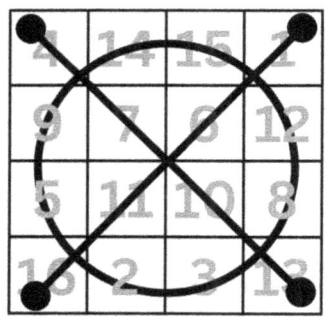

If you want a straightforward number grid without using kamea's, use this 3x3 grid and the Pythagorean numerology table (shown previously).

Intention – **Magic comes easily**.

Remove vowels and repeat letters.

mgcsly = 4,7,3,1,3 &7

Rotating your shape is always interesting, it might resemble a deckchair, baby bouncer or a slide. You can recall the experience of using one of these to charge your sigil.

## Sigil Wheel

A sigil wheel (or witch's wheel) is another way of using a grid to construct a sigil. Its loosely based upon a Rose Cross wheel which uses Hebrew letters and favoured by practitioners of high magic. This more accessible version uses three concentric circles containing the twenty-six letters of the alphabet. Both images are taken from the excellent website *chaostarot.com*.

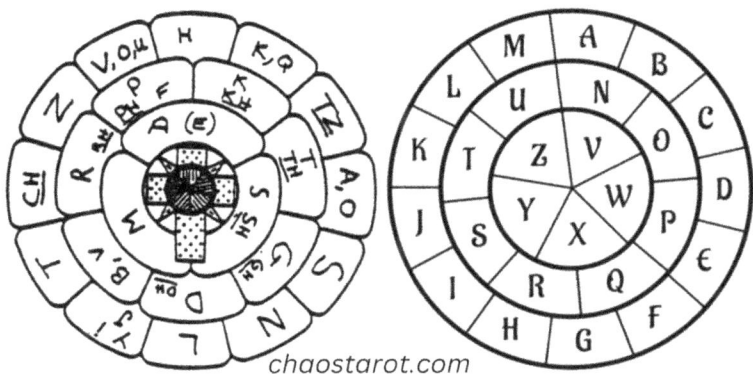

*chaostarot.com*

Not surprisingly magical purists are not very complimentary about the modern variant, despite the words of Hebrew scholar and biblical author St Paul *'to the pure all things are pure'* (Titus 1:15). Sigils are simply tools for results.

Using the sigil wheel to create '**I excel in magic**' sigil.

The completed sigil is encased in a pentagram.

Any sigil that relates to acquisition of magical skills that will make you an effective magician could be physically drawn on yourself. Blood works well in this process as it contains the essence of your life force, your DNA and ancestral line. The idea that something you excel in is 'in your blood' - is very pertinent to this sigil. Obviously obtaining blood requires some thought and hygiene, so a small antiseptic wipe and a clean pin are useful. If you can obtain a diabetic finger pricker, even better. If you are a woman who menstruates, you can collect this with a moon cup rather than pricking yourself. If you are squeamish, saliva can be used instead of blood.

```
   I AM
MAGICIAN
MAGICIA
 MAGICI
 MAGIC
  MAGI
  MAG
   MA
    M
```

This approach uses a triangular incantation based upon the ancient word Abracadabra. This is loosely translated in Hebrew as 'I will create as I speak' or Aramaic 'I create like the word'. It was often transcribed on an amulet for protection. This image provides a chant prefaced by the intentional statement 'I am'.

Magic is a combination of recognising timely coincidences whilst engaging in experiential study. Create opportunities for a sigil to take effect.

It's worth stating that often the success of sigil magic is not just down to technique, but the ongoing practice of a magician.

## The Cut Up Technique

A creative approach, developed by William Burroughs and Brion Gysin, entails cutting up sentences and randomly rearranged to create a new text. David Bowie, Kurt Cobain, Thom Yorke and Genesis P-Orridge have all used this technique to create lyrics. As a process it has many applications, all aimed at liberating magical consciousness. If you can use an old iron pair of scissors, these will help greatly.

You can use this system to further understand an intentional statement. Here is my example.

**I am uniquely skilled in the art of magic, and it comes naturally to me. I am unhindered by people or events. For all things are my teacher.**

I tried to sum up my intention by including what I know about magic; it is unique and natural (I have always known this). It can be hindered by events and people (a frequent source of irritation), but I can learn from these things, if I remember to.

The whole process from creating the original intention and cutting out each word and then immediately rearranging them, took under 10 minutes. You do not have to use every word.

**Naturally, in things or events, I am the teacher of my art; and uniquely skilled, unhindered people come to me, for I am all magic.**

Notice how the emphasis shifts from the external to the internal; and it attracts the right people to work and learn with. This revealing my subconscious desire. It may not read as well, but it creates a far better outcome.

Magic is an act of the will, a mental change that is reflected or enacted in the material world. This process can be observed, sought out and practiced. Comic book writer, playwright, and magician, Grant Morrison in *Pop Magic* (2008), suggests two interrelated exercises.

> *"As a first exercise in magical consciousness spend five minutes looking at everything around you as if ALL OF IT was trying to tell you something very important. How did that light bulb come to be here exactly? Why does the murder victim in the newspaper have the same unusual surname as your father-in-law? Why did the phone ring, just at that moment and what were you thinking when it did? What is that water stain on the wall of the building opposite? How does it make you feel?*
>
> *Next, relax, go for a walk and interpret everything you see on the way as a message from the Infinite to you. Watch for patterns in the flight of birds. Make oracular sentences from the letters on car number plates. Look at the way buildings move against the skyline. Pay attention to noises on the streets, graffiti sigils, voices cut into rapid, almost subliminal commands and pleas. Listen between the lines. Walk as far and for as long as you feel comfortable in this open state. The more aimless, the more you walk for the pleasure of pure experience, the further into magical consciousness you will be immersed".*

Both these exercises experiment with the idea of a speaking world. Buried within us is the original survival technique - listen to your environment. It matters not if it is a concrete car park, or a canopy of trees in a forest. By taking time out to notice meaning in seemingly random things, the magician strengthens the connection between coincidences. As everything is interconnected and in relational motion, then magic is simply recognizing or observing coincidences. If you can do this, then you are a magician.

As the *Hermes Trismegistus* teaches, *"If you set your foot on this path, you will see it everywhere."*

Observation and acknowledgement are good friends to magicians.

# 6

# Money Sigils – Cash from Chaos magic?

*"A roll of the dice will never abolish chance"* - Étienne Mallarmé

Money is a strange entity. Its absence can create an unbearable cycle of poverty; in excess, an unhelpful addiction that constantly demands more of the same, only bigger and better. We all need money. Can sigil magic create money?

There is an old apocryphal story of a man who tried to become rich by doing a series of magical workings in which he visualized himself handling vast stacks of money. Shortly afterwards he lost his job, and the only job he could get was a position at a bank, where he worked eight hours a day on a modest wage counting vast stacks of other people's money. He had focused on the means, money in his hands, rather than the end goal, a lifestyle of relative wealth and financial comfort. If you do practice practical visualisation it appears to work more effectively when focussed upon a specific object or possession, rather than an abstract energy like money. Money is a slippery thing; it comes and goes.

Several decades ago, I worked some magic to receive five hundred pounds to pay an urgent bill, within a week I unexpectedly received the exact amount from the estate of a deceased family friend. Despite my relief at being able to settle the debt, I was also struck by my potential role in this process. In this instance my godfather had already died months before the executors of his estate released funds, so thankfully I did not feel any sense of responsibility.

How we feel about magic determines its success. Magic may flow in relation to our own sense of congruent reality - in what we can reasonably expect to achieve or accomplish. If you do not believe that you are entitled to possess wealth, you are unlikely ever to truly gain it. Your belief will sabotage any chance of success. Of course, the outcome does depend on how you define wealth. If you have an urgent need for funds, you would be better off finding a 'money buddy' and casting money sigils for each other. I can thoroughly recommend this as a short-term measure. It removes the pressing personal need for funds and refocuses magic to assist a friend in need. Reciprocal or mutual magic removes the debilitating feature of lust for personal results, this is an absolute magic killer when you are broke, with your back against the wall.

There are always situations where we need money, so here is one with a useful clause minimizing any negative outcome.

I have five hundred pounds (no strings attached)

Remove all the vowels and any repeat letters (40 letters reduced to 11 letters):

Hv fndr ps tgc

Play with the letters and overlay/ merge any matching shapes.

**Hv fndr ps tgc**

**FV HNDR PS TG C**

**Fvhndrps tgc**

As with many sigils, they are an organic work in progress. Having 'played' with a design and rotating it I found that it resembled a spinning top. So, you could use a spinning object to charge it -

fidget spinners work well. However, to really activate this sigil you could get far more physical.

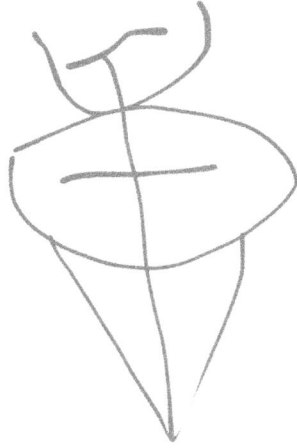

Firstly, ensure you have a clear mental image of your sigil, you will need to picture this throughout this activity. Breathe deeply, gradually increasing in intensity and frequency whilst recalling your sigil. When you are ready start to spin round and continue 'wild dervish' dancing until you can no longer stand – at collapse the sigil is released. Obviously, you should ensure this is a safe activity for you to perform and your working space is suitable, with no obstructions. There are plenty of pre-designed sigils for money available for sale online, although you might wish to consider in this instance, who the actual recipient of this money is!

## Feeling lucky?

I have only once used magic to choose lottery numbers. I bought my ticket towards the end of a remarkable day of beneficial coincidences. I had been interviewed and offered a job I wanted; jumped on a train to London and successfully managed to 'blag' a doorstep interview with an elusive academic and witch for a research project which was on a tight deadline. In this spirit of euphoria, I selected several correct numbers including a bonus number. Amazingly, so too did a great many people, so I won £33. Wherever there are opportunities to gain from chance, there is room for working magic. The chances of winning the jackpot are one in fourteen million and although a well-timed sigil will undoubtedly increase the probability of a win, I suggest there are infinitely more malleable ways of generating money. Start simple with options that have greater probability. Most people have a hobby or interest that gives them the edge when spotting a bargain. I have successfully used sigils to locate bargain finds at car boot sales and antique fairs. If the seller is unwilling to negotiate to accept your offer, suggest flipping a coin (and let them call heads or tails) to determine the outcome. Keep probability on your side. There are plenty of online sites offering auction or 'buy it now' options, where you can resell your purchases.

Lady luck can be a useful ally, throughout history magical talismans, charms when combined with ritual habits are claimed by some to produce successful outcomes. My favourite is to ensure I'm feeling positive, emotionally buoyant, and then clearly recall the image of lining three bells in a row on an old slot machine. If you can 'hear' the sound this makes, so much the better. Good luck!

The Roman Goddess, Fortuna and her Greek counterpart, Tyche were considered arbiters of luck. Both were often depicted blindfolded (blind luck) carrying a symbolic ship's rudder (steering fate), a wheel of fortune, revealing the capricious nature of life and a cornucopia (horn of plenty) symbolising wealth and prosperity. Luck swings both ways and is credited with both good and bad outcomes. Opinions on luck are generally split between pure chance or due to the overruling influence of a sentient being or deity. Personally, my money's on the former, I'm not entirely convinced by the latter. However, if you do discover a benevolent entity who only distributes good luck and fortune, dispense with sigil magic, and become their top devotee.

Modern research into the subject has largely concluded that 'belief in luck' functions like a placebo, creating a positive thought process, which improves people's interpretation of events. This, in part, reflects Carl Jung's idea of synchronicity, where a process of preparation and reflection allows apparent 'coincidences' to become meaningful. Another variant defines luck as 'probability taken personally' which seems rather apt.

Magical potential exists somewhere between possibility and probability. Correctly understood, these key ideas balance, like scales of justice, in everyone. Magic is tipping these scales in your favour, by knowing how (to know) and when, or being alert (to will) to play your hand. Most people drawn to magic are both imaginative and reasonably rational.

Possibility thinking has received a degree of notoriety largely *from a mistaken Christian prosperity gospel, 'if you can conceive it and believe it, you shall receive it'*. Wishful thinking and blind faith make poor partners. However, allowing your creative mind to consider magical possibilities and weighing up the relative probabilities of outcomes are useful skills in sigil magic. Many of us are cautious by nature, however the third section of the witches' pyramid (to dare) encourages courageous action. Magic requires risk taking; not sharing this publicly fulfils the fourth instruction (to keep silent).

Mindset is perhaps the single biggest problem when it comes to creating change. Often our beliefs about money are established quite early on in our development. The childhood experience of watching parents or carers struggling to make ends meet can become a repetitive cycle in our own lives. Thankfully sigil magic can help us reinvent ourselves. Money is important, its absence utterly debilitating. Wealth is an entirely different concept. True wealth is a state of grace or gratitude, a joy of having enough to simply explore and experience life. Wealth is relative to a chosen lifestyle. The key to this puzzle may lie in the last two words. What sort of life do you want? It may seem like a small shift in emphasis but even moving your focus away from the need for money, to an understanding of wealth, can clarify your thinking.

In *Chaotopia* (2006), Dave Lee draws a distinction between these two concepts:

> "*Money is a parameter, whose value is arbitrary and impersonal; wealth is a skill, whose value is arbitrary and*

*personal. Money is a Spirit, an elemental; Wealth is the attribute of a God."*

Don't let the 'g-word' put you off, it's a comparative statement revealing the relative subordination of 'cheap' money to 'liberating' wealth. Lee illustrates this through a simple evaluation by listing twenty things that you regularly enjoy doing. From these, select your top ten activities and ask yourself if you would devote more money to these. From the same list ask a second question, would I devote more time to these? It could look like this:

| Top 10 regular activities | £ | ⧖ |
|---|---|---|
| Reading books | No | Yes |
| Walking in countryside | No | Yes |
| Making love | No | Yes |
| Attending gigs | Yes | Yes |
| Playing sports | No | No |
| Weekend breaks | Yes | No |
| Eating out | Yes | No |
| Spending time with family | No | Yes |
| Bargain hunting | Yes | Yes |
| Watching TV | No | Yes |

Money 60%

Time 30%

In this case the person is spending too much time not doing the things they enjoy with slightly insufficient funds. Invariably, there is a level of discrepancy. It's a useful activity to complete unless, of course, you are already living your best possible life, in which case I would have to question why you are reading this book.

Moving beyond a 'base need' for money can facilitate one of my favourite sigils. Its utterly pragmatic, as it doesn't limit wealth to money derived from hours worked, or even employment.

## MONEY COMES EASILY TO ME

You can remove vowels and repeat letters leaving the letters m n y c l t remaining. These can be merged to give you a variation of the first design. This might be simplified to the second, which is easier to picture and draw in a mild trance state. In a different way this could be conjured in your mind as a pair of crossed trumpets with accompanying sounds.

  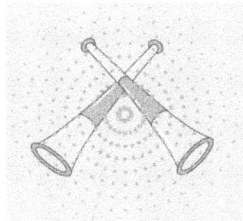

To further charge your sigil, enter a light trance and imagine a 3D image of your sigil. Picture the shape in led rope lights, that light up in sequence like a Mexican wave running around your sigil. Gradually expand this shape until it is big enough for you to step inside. Imagine yourself inside your sigil and enjoy the experience of being surrounded or encapsulated by your intention that 'money comes easily to me'. Try this every day for a month.

When money is exchanged within communities it can benefit many people, the more times it changes hands, the more useful it is. Removing it from circulation and amassing it dormant in offshore accounts defeats the whole process. The legitimization of this process through the exploitation of tax loopholes is one of the most impoverishing features of modern society. The bulk of wealth generated provides no community benefit, neither is it taxable to regenerate healthcare or education. Companies become reward providers for shareholders and executives, relegating customers to second or third place. Many water companies exemplify this by regularly polluting customers coastlines with impunity, as it is cheaper to eventually pay fines than reinvest profits and risk shareholder revolt.

The average occultist or magician's attitude to macroeconomics and active retaliation to the prospect of financial impoverishment is seldom discussed, as Gordon White in *Chaos Protocols* (2020) wryly notes.

> '*Learning about demons is just more fun than learning about consumer price inflation, even though only one of the is absolutely guaranteed to negatively affect your life*'.

Using money as sigils has a long and illustrious history. I recently visited *"Defaced! Money, Conflict, Protest"* at The Fitzwilliam Museum in Cambridge, its strapline from contributor Mark Wagner, '*If you're fed up and throwing rocks isn't your thing, take it out on money*" immediately caught my eye. The exhibition featured examples of defaced and mutilated currency from Roman times through to the French and American revolutions and more recent Suffragette and Black Lives Matter movements. It made for a fascinating exhibition. Frequently satirizing politicians and monarchs defaced hard cash was passed through multiple hands, just like sigils circulating symbols of protest. In a world increasingly controlled by digital currency and facing a cost-of-living crisis, hard cash is the last resort of personal autonomy. The absence of a digital footprint protects anonymity. Perhaps it is already too late to change this. Personally, I'm quite happy to use a mixture of both. I'm not happy to let economic policies set by the eye-wateringly-rich oppress and diminish the wealth of the rest of us. This time next year we are unlikely to be millionaires, so cast some sigils, *you know it makes sense, Rodney*!

# 7
# SIGILS FOR PROTECTION

*"The best lightning rod for your protection is your own spine"* - Ralph Waldo Emerson

The evolution of humanity has birthed various symbols associated with protection. They are easily observed today and have kept jewellers in business throughout the ages. In a real sense the history of ideas (and perhaps fears) is reflected through them.

Take a walk down any urban high street and you will find Crosses, Pentagrams, Stars of David, Hamsa hands, St Christopher emblems, Ankhs, Celtic knots, Runes and even shark's teeth, displayed by passers-by. This symbolic association connects the wearer to concepts considerably greater than the sum of its parts. Some regard them as religious emblems, symbols of divine protection from evil, or images that provide a link beyond death into eternity. The fear of hidden dangers, predatory evil or separation from 'God', plays unnerving mind-games in the human psyche, even though it's a very long time since any sharks infested Wimbledon high street.

These images are sigils and maybe talismans too. You can incorporate any similar symbols into your own sigil for protection. Whilst many people have rejected any overtly religious association, these symbols remain powerful images. As society changes, new fears and challenges emerge. Sigils remain potent tools for protection.

Sigils for protection as apotropaic marks are often found in old buildings, located on doors, floors, windows, chimneys, and fireplaces. These reflect fears arising from the presence of malevolent magic and are designed to seal possible points of entry. One common design contains hexafoils, overlapping circles with flower motifs, designed to confuse malevolent spirits.

Another striking design requested protection from the Virgin Mary as *Virgo Virginum*. These sigil marks contain the initials VM or VV crisscrossed and etched or burnt into stone or wood, to ward off evil. In 2019, over a hundred were discovered in a cave at Creswell Crags in Nottinghamshire. The majority focus upon a dark, deep chasm at the end of the cave, it can an unnerving site to visit.

You could incorporate your version of these designs in a sigil.

Most practitioners of magic recognise the concept of boundaries as partitions of protection. A magical working space, however constructed, both creates and crosses over boundaries. Liminal spaces as borderlands provide opportunities for magic. These are the realms of the *haegtessa*, an old Saxon work for hedge or boundary crosser, that defined the English word 'witch'. Of course, many practitioners of magic might not identify as a witch, it's still a great descriptor for magic and a reminder that 'boundary pushing' is a function of sigil magic. This crossing over occurs when a sigil, created by the conscious mind is flipped into the unconscious mind.

The 'idea of boundaries' is a popular theme in modern thought, promoted by influencers and life coaches as *'invisible partitions, reminding others where they stop and where you begin'*. Consequently, personal boundaries are seen as a sign of emotional maturity, their absence, leads to the fear of being trampled over by others. Perhaps this is culture catching up with magic, most of us have had to deal with people who consistently drain our energy. Protection enables us to choose who to let in and who to keep out. For many of us this contains a level of trial and error, it's always easy to be wise after the event. Historically, boundaries have related to land and possessions, the internalisation of these ideas in relation to relationships, is considerably more complex. Exploring appropriate boundaries between intimacy and possessiveness, without treating others as objects, is worthy of time and effort.

Every now and again we encounter situations that threaten our well-being and perhaps our very survival. Under these circumstances a sigil is extremely helpful, particularly if you don't have a blasting stick to hand.

Symbolic representations of protection sigils as charms, amulets, and talismans have been used to ward off evil throughout history.

One of the most famous, is the Norse rune Œgishjalmr, better known as the Helm of Awe or Fear helm. It appears within an untitled, anonymous collection of Scandinavian poems, known nowadays as the *Poetic Edda*.

> "The fear-helm I wore to afright mankind,
> While guarding my gold I lay.
> Mightier seemed I than any man,
> For a fiercer never I found".

This symbol is believed to strike terror into anyone attempting to attack you your family and loved ones or your possessions. It's a great standalone sigil. It comprises of a circular series of repeat images, you could include one of the strands into a personalised sigil. For example, as a pictorial representation of yourself, encapsulated in a modern 'no entry' symbol.

I am shielded from nightmares

A shield is also a great design to incorporate into a sigil. Shields can be used for both defence and attack.

With all sigils it's important to allow your imagination free flow when you reduce your statement to create your graphic representation of intent.

Some sigils, and protection sigils are a good example, can be retained rather than burnt or buried. If they are placed in an obvious place where you will regularly see them, your conscious mind will gradually filter out its presence until only your unconscious mind will recognise it. That said, you may wish to set a reminder on your phone to recharge your sigil at regular intervals, if required.

Whilst considering a puzzling conundrum, I became aware that a particular person would probably lie about their involvement in this matter. As often in these situations, I could neither prove it, nor did I wish to be in a position where I wrongly accused them. Intuition is a remarkable tool for insight, its value lies in how you apply it. I very much doubted that the individual concerned would ever own up to being the source of the rumour. Consequently, I needed a sigil that would facilitate the individual freely volunteering that they were present during a specific conversation. It worked well, the individual backtracked on three occasions and conceded that they were present. Magic can sometimes tread a fine line between another's freewill and a little bit of helpful engineering by the magician.

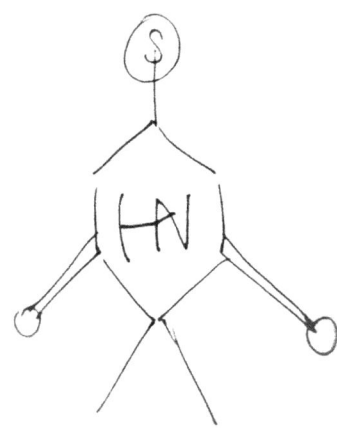

The sigil is loosely based upon the chemical arrangement of Sodium Pentothal, the alleged 'truth drug' used for obtaining otherwise hidden information. Its efficacy is distinctly questionable, however due to its use in spy films portraying the Cold war era, it carries its own memory in people's minds. Sigils only need a loose connection to the magician to be effective. The initials of the individual are hidden in the image, which rather helpfully resembles a stick person. Some sigils simply require an original thought.

Sometimes a protection sigil requires an extra push of energy. Several years ago, I was asked to create a sigil to protect a property and its occupants from a particular individual, who had been threatening and aggressive towards the household.

The owner of the property had changed the locks and installed an intruder alarm system. A sigil was created to protect the property and occupants, which was then redrawn in felt marker on a mirror. The sigil was then charged, and a photo of the miscreant was reflected in the mirror bearing the sigil. As we felt the energy rise, I smashed the mirror with a small hammer. This released the sigil to quite dramatic effect. Every alarm in the house went off and dogs along the street started barking. So much for 'to be silent'.

If you replicate this using a mirror, be sure to either place it in a clear plastic bag or wrap in it cling film, to prevent any stray shards of glass causing harm.

Binding danger is a significant aspect of sigil magic. It is an effective method for preventing 'a greater harm'. My favourite is derived from a four-thousand-year-old Babylonian text. My version reads as follows,

By the command of *Marduk* (*Martuch*) the Lord of Dreams, Master of Bewitchment,

> *"With ropes I will entwine,*
> *As in a cage I will catch.*
> *As with cords I will tie.*
> *As in a net I will overpower.*
> *As in a sling, I will twist and tear like fabric.*
> *With dirty water from a well I will fill.*
> *As a wall I will throw them down".*

I have used this within knot magic, with a total of seven knots tied for each statement. Nevertheless, it can also be incorporated into a sigil design. You could use a key descriptor from each statement and condense them, alternatively you could use the pictorial method in the following way.

Take the key images from the text an either hand draw a representation of them or select them from a clip art package. I have done the latter; I really wouldn't inflict my art on you.

Entwined Rope
Caught in a cage
Tied cords
Overpowered by a net
Twisted sling
Filled with dirty water
Thrown from a wall

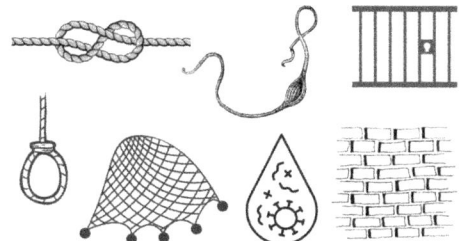

These images are then superimposed which creates a rather hectic picture. Personally, I prefer to simplify this further as in the middle image, which then is redrawn in the picture on the right, revealing the recipient swinging in a cage.

# 8
# INTENTION AND ETHICS IN MAGIC

*"Most occultists are reconciled to the idea that many of their most cherished sets of symbols and practices may well only be methods of 'slight of mind'"* - Julian Vayne

Magic as a system or process for change, seems to work within independently of any ethical framework. Just like water, it flows along the path of least resistance. It can be considered morally neutral. However, an act of magic to influence another person or alter an outcome, carries personal responsibility for the magician. How does the magician decide whether a particular sigil is an appropriate, or moral use of magic? Whether we like it or not, our magic is influenced by our ethics.

Unless you are a sociopath, most people behave according to a moral compass. This acts like an internal gauge approximately in line with the expectations of society. Naturally people experience this differently with varying degrees of compliance. Casting a sigil for an outcome you believe is questionable is going to undermine your magic.

For thousands of years ethics has focussed on divine commands, like the ten commandments of Judaism and Christianity. Doing 'the right thing' is following god's revealed will in a holy book. Fine if that's your thing, although most sacred texts contain frustratingly conflicting instructions. To avoid these discrepancies and the need for a particular statement of faith, philosopher Emmanuel Kant (1724 –1804) attempted to create a hierarchy of first principles. These instructions can be positive or negative. 'Do not steal' becomes socially preferable to 'always steal'. However, there are always exceptions to rules, perhaps a pressing need to feed your family. Later developments considered the utilitarian consequences of actions through maximizing pleasure or minimizing pain. This shifts the focus away from a good intention to a positive outcome. Ask any experienced magician, or moral philosopher for that matter, outcomes can be notoriously difficult to accurately predict.

The prospect of altering events to the advantage of the magician is as alluring to the practitioner as it is as unsettling to the public. Fear of black magic, witchcraft and other forms of sorcery seem to resurface during times of social upheaval or crisis. Conspiracy theories are not just a modern feature of a media-driven society. During a five-year period between 184-179 BCE and long before the birth of Christianity, five thousand people were sentenced to death by magistrates in the Roman Empire, convicted for practicing magic. Two thousand years later during the 1980's and early 90's the satanic panic gripped America and Britain. Fundamentalist Christian therapists used coercive and suggestive interrogation to gain uncorroborated statements from children. Many of these were used to convince social services to take children into care from parents who were rumoured to magicians and witches. Abuse, whether committed within the confines of church, youth association, sports or educational setting is abuse, its context largely irrelevant. For a decade the media, charities, schools, and police colluded in this fabrication demonizing practitioners of magic. It prompted over 12,000 unsubstantiated cases of Satanic ritual abuse. Ironically, the forceable removal of children from their families on such spurious grounds, was the real instance of abuse. There are many who would wish these events to remain firmly in the past, however increasingly authoritarian governments need scapegoats, which the media are (largely) obliged to vilify. The spectre of unreasonable persecution remains.

Several theories have been proposed to maintain the moral action of the magician, with varying levels of success. Most people reading this will have encountered some of them.

The '*Law of Threefold Return*' claims that the consequences of any magical act are returned upon the magician or witch three times over. It's a common belief amongst some witches and many wiccans and is referenced in the writings of Gerald Gardner. In its original setting, this view specifically refers to the relationship between a more experienced witch and their initiate. It reminds the student to return good to their mentor three times over as an act of gratitude. It is expressed within a particular context and entirely positive. It doesn't say '*if you do bad things, bad things will happen to you*'. It has no negative formulation.

Some have suggested that the law of threefold return can be used as a universal principle for all magic, claiming if you pursue magic for good, good will be returned threefold. Equally the opposite would apply. There may be some merit in this view in considering the outcome of magic upon the practitioner. Intentional magic has a habit of rubbing off, malevolent harmful results may well negatively affect the person working magic. Of course, this would also be true for positive, beneficial magic. However, as Doreen Valiente observed, it is difficult to quantify the idea of 'three-fold' in a particular situation and didn't think it was fair to apply this idea to witches.

Moving even further from its original formulation, some have linked the law of threefold return to modern Western ideas about Karma. This appears to remove Karma from its Vedic location. Within its original setting, Karma applies to actions appropriate to a fixed, hereditary caste system. Hindus are born into a fixed role within society with clear parameters defining responsibilities and expectations. Actions that uphold this structure are considered beneficial to society and are rewarded with good karma and vice versa. A positive outcome could be an ordered society. On the other hand, as Gandhi suspected, it could simply be an unjust means of social control, maintaining a karmic glass ceiling. The stated goal of good karma is to escape the endless cycle of birth and rebirth and achieve moksha, negative karma hinders this release, leading to a less favourable existence in a future life. Thus, the application of karma influences a multitude of incarnations, rather than necessarily producing an instant result in a single lifetime.

When taken out of context, the Law of Threefold return combined with a simplistic view of Karma, can lead to misunderstanding. We can easily observe that frequently the idle rich grow increasingly wealthy at the expense of the hardworking poor. The gap between rich and poor continues to grow disproportionately. Unless karma is capitalist, our experience and the poverty people face disproves these ideas. Neither idea provides any real solace for those currently suffering hardship. You may be able to improve your life, but ultimately you only get what you deserve. If you are uncomfortable by my ideological perspective, I hope you will acknowledge that neither the Law of Threefold return nor Karmic outcomes are universally observed laws. Gravity would be a much better example of this.

The Wiccan Rede is another idea influencing the morality of magic and was proposed by Doreen Valiente in 1964. It reads as follows; *'Eight words the Wiccan Rede fulfill, an it harm none, do what ye will'*. A 'rede' is an advisory statement and less restrictive than a law. It introduces a broad instruction 'do no harm' as a first duty (echoing Kant). However, the *'harm none'* principle is as profound as it is perplexing. Our very existence harms something, whether we eat meat or not. It requires measuring the impact of our magic, like considering the impact of ripples in water or intentional tugs of the web of the wyrd. Magic is justified within the final four words *'do what ye will'*. It's not saying, do whatever you like, but asks, *is this action indicative of my explored magical will*? If it does, you act with integrity and goodness - in accordance with your revealed nature. This leads back to our working definition of magic as *'the art and science of changing consciousness at will'*.

It may be that none of these examples appeals to you. It might appear that none of these largely theoretical ideas carry little impact in everyday sigil magic. However, few of us can step beyond our self-defined moral framework. Our upbringing and cultural expectations, creates a desire to do the right thing, or at least to be seen to do the right thing. Our stated beliefs or those buried in our unconscious mind will influence any magical working, regardless of our intention. When we attempt magic that compromises our true will, invariably, we self-sabotage the outcome.

Personally, my moral code for practical magic is best described as 'reciprocal magic of the will'. It's a variation of the 'golden rule' and summed up in the statement, *'Only work magic you are prepared to have worked on you'*. This always includes benevolent sigils like healing, as I would naturally wish that for myself. It also allows working magic to produce favourable changes in my circumstances. It prohibits manipulative love sigils on unwitting individuals. I have no wish for that in my life. It allows for binding sigils on those who pose a genuine threat to themselves or others. If I ever met these criteria, I trust my magical friends would bind me. There are plenty of occasions when I have worked magic, casting sigils to inhibit and restrict others, provided my action is to prevent *'a greater harm'*, my conscience is clear and magic flows.

## Congruence in action

A good example of acting with congruency is found in the in the Hebrew bible in the third book of the Neviim. The story of David and Goliath is often presented as the triumph of the underdog over the might of a reigning champion. That is if you have never really read the story.

You can more commonly find it in the Old Testament in the first book of Samuel chapter 17.

David, a shepherd, is taking supplies to a battlefield where his eleven older brothers are in service to king Saul. The Israelites are at war with the Philistines. Both armies occupy hill tops, the valley between them the battlefield. The sides of the valley were very steep. Whoever made the first move would have a strong disadvantage and probably suffer great loss, consequently, both sides were waiting for the other to attack first.

For forty days the Philistine giant Goliath mocked the Israelite army. Upon hearing this, David persuades the king to let him fight Goliath. Saul gives David his armour and weapons. David rejects these, preferring a slingshot and a few stones from a local riverbed. There is an exchange of insults from both David and Goliath before David drops Goliath with a single shot and chops off his head with Goliath's own sword. There is little doubt that David was certain of this outcome. The Hebrew text describes Goliath as being led around by guides, his movement and vision restricted by probable gigantism. Stealth and surprise meant that David never got close enough to be vulnerable to attack from Goliath. Local knowledge ensured that the stones chosen were high density volcanic rock unique to this location and quite capable of stunning or killing. David's approach was consistent with his shepherding skills and supported by his beliefs.

David's victory is memorialized within the hexagram, the compound of two congruent triangles of the Star of David, in Hebrew דָּוִד מָגֵן also called David's shield. Significantly the physical shield offered by king Saul was rejected by David. Thus David's shield is a metaphor, the timely alignment of his sense of entitlement, his belief in the divine and empathy towards the plight of his people. The compound of these two congruent triangles, the hexagram, the agreement, ensured his success. Within this harmony, magic flows easily. Remember, belief in a particular god, is only useful if it helps achieve the outcome of your sigil.

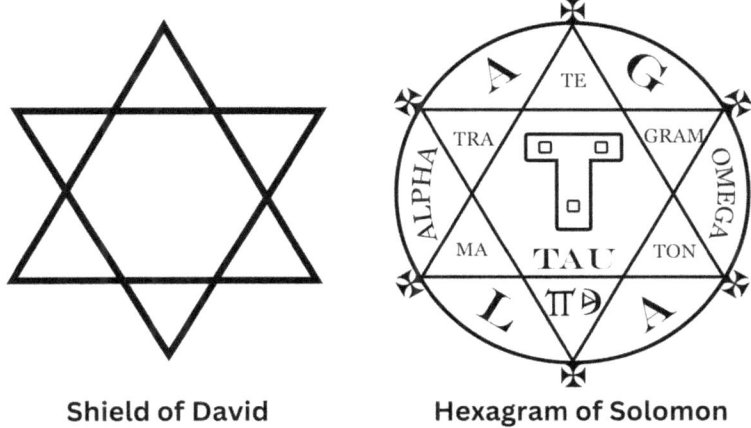

**Shield of David**     **Hexagram of Solomon**

In magical thought, the hexagram mirrors an exchange of consciousness. The upward triangle representing the ascension of consciousness, the downward, the descent of matter into physical realms. Also within this image are the symbols of the element of water (downward triangle) and the element of fire (upward triangle). As these align the element of earth (downward triangle with line) and the element of Air (upward triangle with line) appear.

Magical thought has many of such conjunctions. The phrase 'as above so below' is understood by many to represent the alignment of higher and natural energies. Its full citation within the writings of Hermes Trismegistus is *"As above, so below, as within, so without, as the universe, so the soul."* This reveals a necessary alignment between the interior experience and external projection of the magician. Rather than a passive acceptance of 'what will be, will be' - the responsibility lies with the individual to pursue a path of authenticity in accordance with their will.

The *Gospel of Thomas* was rediscovered near Nag Hammadi, near Egypt in December 1945. Its arguably one the earliest collections of the sayings of Jesus and contains more detailed accounts of the childhood of Jesus than other gospels. It was rejected by the church during the reign of Constantine around 300 CE, and thus avoided inclusion in the canon of the modern Bible which developed during the 4$^{th}$ century CE. It contains a similar hidden or gnostic message mirroring this same idea of alignment.

> *"When you make the two into one, and when you make the inner like the outer and the outer like the inner, and the upper like the lower, and when you make male and female into a single one... then you will enter [the kingdom]."*

I must admit this regularly makes me chuckle, imagine the outrage this idea would cause amongst the 'religious right' in America and elsewhere, when interpreted literally. Magic can be found in both humour and the symmetries between inner and outer landscapes when our intention is synonymous with our will. This congruence is achieved by true alignment, existing in agreement. It has its own symbol ≅ which can be included within a sigil to strengthen its outcome.

Many historic sigils are based upon a variation of the hexagram.

The hexagram, as with many magical symbols, can be used to strengthen a sigil, forming a powerful border surrounding your design.

# 9
# Further Techniques

*"Symbols are to the mind, what tools are to the hand, an extended application of its powers" - Dion Fortune*

I hope by now you will have concluded that successful sigil magic is the product of a healthy mindset and a creative imagination. We all choose our belief narratives and repeat stories to ourselves about who we are and how we inhabit the world around us. When this is aligned with a unique and artisan understanding of your personal will, in relation to possibilities and probabilities, within an interconnected and ever-changing universe, sigil magic is highly effective.

Most sigils have a singular purpose. They require minimal preparation and can be constructed, charged, and released within a short timeframe. However, some magic requires a more complex sigil formulation. It could be that several interrelated events need to occur before the desired outcome is complete. This can be achieved in several ways.

Perhaps the easiest technique is to design several sigils on transparent acetate or good old-fashioned tracing paper. You could create a composite sigil by overlaying them and redrawing the new design. Alternately, only redraw the shape that only corresponds in all your overlapping sigils.

Another approach is like the first time you wrote your signature. To begin it was a clearly defined piece of writing, however with the passage of time, most people's signature resembles a squiggle, with hardly any resemblance to your actual name, yet it still carries the same authority. You can use this with an existing sigil you have created which you redraw by hand, faster and faster until it is completely redesigned and *voila* - a new sigil.

Many magicians, including Spare, created their own personal symbols (or correspondences) to reflect ongoing aspirations, which can be incorporated within other sigils in many different contexts. Donald Michael Kraig in *Modern Magick* (2010) notes how this technique applies to almost abstract qualities, such as peace, hope love and desire. Their value lies in their unique relationship to your experience. For example, consider how you might illustrate hope, you might picture this as an anchor, remember, the actual image is only useful in so much as it as it resonates with you. Begin by drawing an anchor and then redraw it repeatedly, steadily increasing your speed until you have reduced it down to a unique shape. This process, when performed with intent, will lodge the final shape in your subconscious mind. Thus, this shape will always summon hope, however you use it. You can use this approach to create your own sigil alphabet of desire.

## Using a simple memory tool to create a sigil

The following example uses an acrostic, where the first letter of each word creates another word. It's an excellent exam revision technique and a great way to create a sigil.

Say, for example, you are attracted to someone who has a bad experience with a previous partner. This naturally makes them cautious, so you want to reassure them of your integrity.

Create a list of things or qualities you want them to recognise and find attractive in you. Include a mixture of characteristics then narrow these down to ten.

Try to use single words as this makes the mnemonic easier to create.

**Approachable**

**Natural**

**Tantalising**

**Outgoing**

**Intriguing**

**Captivating**

**Relxed**

**Thoughtful**

**Trustworthy**

**Appealing**

In this case the first letter of each quality spells the word 'attraction'.

You could simply use this word or cut it down by removing the vowels and repeat letters to leave the remaining letters, **t r c n**.

You could chant this as an approximation of 'traction' in relation to your goal moving forward.

Alternatively, if the first letters of each word don't create a new mnemonic as a word, you could create a sigil like the example shown, which simply takes the first letter of each quality and removing vowels and repeat letters and overlaps letters until you are pleased with the design. The ten outward arrows signify each of your characteristics impressing (or reassuring) the person concerned.

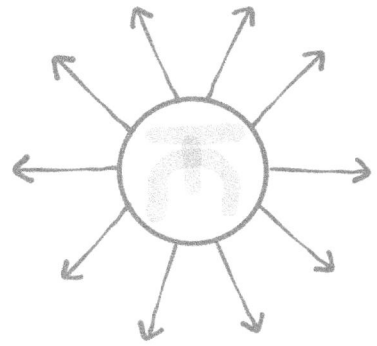

## Sigils as Mnemotechnic Devices

Perhaps the oldest method for the storage and retrieval of information was pioneered in ancient Roman and Greek culture as the method of *Loci* (location). This technique enabled orators to structure and communicate ideas and information at ease without relying on reading from notes. Specific details are transferred or encoded into a physical location well-known to the speaker, who mentally walks around the place recalling the details. More recently the memory of loci has been called the memory journey, memory palace or mind palace technique. Arthur Conan Doyle's original Sherlock Holmes referred to this as the brain attic, the BBC series *Sherlock* makes frequent use of this technique, as does Patrick Jane in the Mentalist.

The application of this approach provides the inclusion of multiple information and is suitable for a complex sigil. You can use any image of a place well known to you, especially if you can picture yourself moving around it. It can be helpful to use the memory of a house with multiple rooms and at least one staircase to facilitate your sigil 'going up a level' or entering a higher phase.

Spend some time working on your overall intention, you can create several statements of outcome. Always elect the one that excites you the most! Consider the necessary steps that need to occur to manifest your outcome. Don't worry about generating too much information at this stage or about being too specific, just get going and make sure you have plenty of paper to write everything down. Once you have lots of ideas, you can group them sequentially using a mind-map, editing them as you go along. The next phase is to allocate or embed each selected idea within objects within each room. Select a prominent item like a chair, table, lamp fitting, rug, mirror, or bed. It helps if you can really 'feel' each object, if you can enter a mild trance and 'name' or mark each item with an intention, this will make the process simpler. Remember to use doors, doorways and a staircase attaching the sensation of moving through them to your intention. This shouldn't take too long as an initial task, maybe spending no more than thirty to forty minutes per day as you work through each room. The trick here is to ensure you can clearly remember each object used, so practice your recall, as you picture moving through each room as a regular revision activity. You might find you can complete the house within a week.

You can create a simple ritual to activate your mental sigil, this could be as simple as burning or burying your overall intention statement. To charge the sigil regularly imagine walking around the house, noticing the objects whilst remaining oblivious to (or deliberately ignoring) the intentions attached to them. Complete this as a regular activity to bring your sigil to completion.

Alternatively, if your intention is 'to pass your exams' simply use the mind palace to retain necessary information for academic success.

There really is no limit to the complexity of advanced sigils. The first humble barcode appeared in 1952 as a visual representation of data using thick and thin bars, based upon morse code. It took over twenty years of development to become commercially viable. By 1982, Christian conspiracy theorists, influenced by Mary Stewart Relfe's book *The New Money System 666*, claimed barcodes contained the number of the Beast, signifying the mark of the Antichrist. Despite its dubious exegesis, I suspect it made the author a lot of money. Barcodes are everywhere, scanned and read, quicker than a blink of the eye. They are perhaps the ultimate sigil, an image that is completely unrecognizable and removed from the information it carries.

There are plenty of free software applications, so you could create a sigil as a barcode.

This took about three minutes to create, my intention was 'all will work out' which was translated into numbers using the Pythagorean numerology table from chapter 5.

## BARCODE #
## 13359335692632

For a more complex sigil or series of sigils the intentional statements can be reduced by the removal of vowels and repeat letters and then converting the remaining letters to numbers.

This example relates to an internal promotion.

- My boss will acknowledge my talents.
- I will be invited to interview.
- I will be calm and relaxed.
- I have the promotion.
- I am invincible.

The first four intentions are condensed, by vowel and repeat letter removal and the remaining fifteen letters are converted into a barcode:

The fifth intention 'I am invincible' is converted into a sigil and overlaid on the rotated barcode:

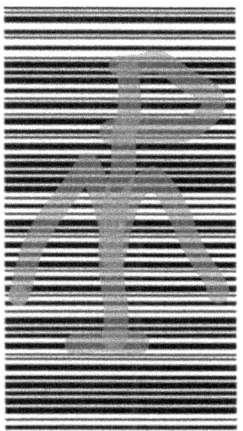

I'm always fascinated by the application of natural phenomena to magic. Another popular example uses the collective interaction of fish (and other aquatic animals), known as shoaling. According to Fisheries Research at the Biodiversity Laboratory, St Joseph's University, shoaling fish enjoy a greater success in finding food and potential mates. Significantly, they possess greater protection from predators, in a shoal of a hundred fish, everyone has only a one-in-one-hundred chance of being killed during an attack. The confusion effect suggests that a predator, confronted with a large group of similar-looking individuals, experiences perceptual confusion, which slows the attack. This may occur because the predator has difficulty identifying a single individual fish to attack.

It's an interesting analogy to apply to sigil casting. Gordon White, in his blog, Rune Soup defines shoaling as

> *'The deployment of multiple, interrelated sigils in the one activation session'.*

In practice, this entails choosing your ultimate objective or outcome and breaking it down into smaller goals. Find the statement that best imbodies your goal, often an intuitive response (check for goosebumps) and break it down into three interconnected statements of intent. Then create a sigil for each one. Shoaling in the natural world is an entirely relational activity between individual fish with each other, which builds upwards to a collective expression.

White outlines three basic principles of shoaling.

- Each member maintains a minimum distance from other objects in its environment, including other members.
- Each member matches the velocity of its neighbour.
- Each member moves toward the perceived centre of the mass.

It's a great example of interactive interrelated activity that can be utilized for sigils for magic.

A further development suggested by White is the introduction of a 'robofish'. In 2010, biologists from the University of Leeds used a computer-controlled replica fish to successfully influence and set the pace within a shoal of fish. In a magical context a robofish is a sigil of an outcome that is guaranteed, for example *'I clean my teeth each morning'*. It requires no specific magic, simply a desire for regular, daily oral hygiene. There are endless permutations for this approach, *'the sun will rise today'* or *'I will wake up and desire coffee'* are easily achieved sigils. Thus, the presence of a robofish sigil as an inevitable outcome elicits a similar successful outcome amongst the other sigils. Job done. Shoaling seems to support Peter J Carroll's observation that seemingly small incremental changes influence events, however improbably, towards your stated intention.

The following example uses five broad statements including a robofish sigil.

- I choose the projects I work on and they succeed.
- My friends and family are happy, my dog is healthy.
- My solicitors work quickly, cheaply and get the job done.
- I experience good luck and financial benefit in all I do.
- Today and every day, dawn will proceed dusk.

Remove vowels and repeat letters and align the remaining fourteen letters in the sigil wheel.

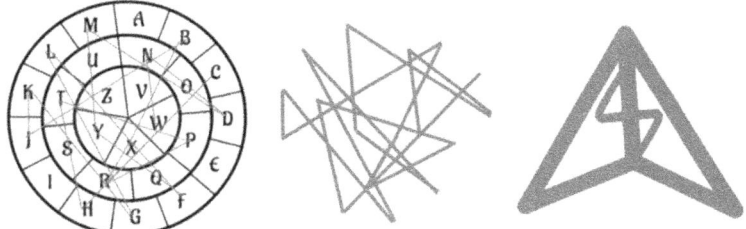

This creates a rather complex design.
It is further reduced until a 'pleasing' design emerges.

# 10
# How does magic work?

*"The soul is the ancestral animals. The body is their knowledge" - Austin Osman Spare*

It's safe to assume that you are still reading this book because you have or wish to experience magic. There are several different perspectives as to exactly how (or perhaps why), magic works. One, perhaps the most popular, suggests that it's possible to unlock hidden or occult abilities, latent in specific individuals, through specific learnt techniques. This could entail years of study within a particular tradition, culminating in the revelation of arcane knowledge or enlightenment.

There are two approaches to this process. Both broadly follow the working definition of magic as *'the art or science of changing consciousness at will'*. This concentrates on 'inner work' realigning the will of the magician to create a greater flow of insight and magic. For some, the will is to become 'one with the divine' through the dissolution of the ego. Others see this in more individual terms of becoming a living 'god' sometimes called attaining apotheosis. These can appear as very different, almost opposite outcomes. They are sometimes referred to respectively (and perhaps dualistically) as right-hand and left-hand paths. The former relies upon basic precepts expressed through societies, lodges, and formal covens with differing levels of hierarchy. The latter, the left-hand path, may have collective expressions, but is a largely individualistic affair. Both these different approaches provide routes to understanding magic but require considerable time and effort.

In contrast to these approaches, some witches and psychics claim they were born with a hereditary 'gift' which is selectively, sometimes secretly, passed down through a family bloodline.

The problem with all these explanations stems from their exclusivity; not all of us can devote years to study or are aware of an influencing ancestor or fairy godmother. Magic is bigger than any singular approach.

To effect change by will is a universal human experience, whether expressed through art, science, religion, or magic. It's an essential component of 'being human'. Our emergence as a species, with a developing consciousness, was as result of recognising relationships, anticipating events, and taking action to meet basic needs. This was expressed in early sigils and cave art in an ever-changing, sometimes hostile, animated world. This early example may well provide some answers.

Consider an example from early humanity, when confronted with a dilemma it is perfectly reasonable to assume an answer might be sought from the security of a local landmark, an old tree, a rock outcrop on a hilltop, or a body of water. In this context it is highly probable that an answer was heard as an audible voice, a theme developed by Julian Jaynes in *The Origin of Human Consciousness in the Breakdown of the Bicameral Mind* (1976). Whilst I wouldn't agree with many of his themes, it is significant in establishing the idea of a speaking landscape. In modern usage this idea is described as animism, described by Dr Graham Harvey in Listening People Speaking Earth (1997) as a recognition that *"the natural world is a community of living persons, only some of whom are human"*. Over the last hundred years Western philosophy has wrestled with these ideas, leading to a reappraisal of animal rights. Originally these ideas highlighted the pain caused to animals through human indifference to their suffering, this has been extended to recognising *'an equal consideration of interests'* in how humans treat animals and how animals feel within this experience. Central to this view is the idea of sentience, many natural beings express the ability to will, or fulfil a specific purpose.

Ecological philosophy has expanded sentience to include natural things, rocks, rivers, and trees attributing them with dynamic purpose. For example, rivers considered sacred by our ancestors, have a desire to flow. This also includes places, landscapes, and ecosystems. In a similar but different way, it can be extended to political or religious belief systems and anything that might be considered 'a community of intention'.

This is a significant departure from early definitions of animism. Nineteenth century anthropologist, Sir Edward Tylor viewed animism as a 'primitive state', the first stage in an evolutionary progression from polytheism into a 'civilised' monotheist Christian society. Significantly, Tylor differed from his contemporaries in defining animism as an early belief system, rather than an early attempt at natural classification. In a similar vein, Swiss psychologist Jean Piaget considered animism an early stage in child development, evidenced by a childlike ability to interact with toys as living beings with feelings. Both Tylor and Piaget considered animism to be an immature, but necessary, aspect of human development. It's not hard to critique these traditional views with their hierarchy of ideas, many might rightly claim many aspects of modern society are anything but civilised. Likewise, the largest example of monotheism requires a 'childlike faith' in an invisible and sometimes capricious god.

> 'Unless you change and become like little children, you will never enter the kingdom of heaven'.
>
> Jesus [cited in Matthew 18:3 NIV]

A broad application of animism provides an inclusive and universal understanding of a diverse community which recognises a family of relationships. It's a remarkably insightful worldview which can include complex beliefs about spirits and gods in a more traditional context, or simply interpret these differently as interdependent, interactive natural phenomena.

Any consideration of how or why magic works, moves animism from an early explanation of natural events to a process to influence the cause and outcome of events. Blurring the edges between natural and metaphysical realms seems a good place to start, particularly if neither are seen as mutually exclusive.

These ideas were popularised in *The Way of the Wyrd* (2004) where Professor Brian Bates provides a fictional account set in 6th Century England, depicting the interaction between a Christian monk as he encounters Anglo-Saxon pagan beliefs. It deals with differing ideas about the interaction of fate and destiny, magic, and beliefs, within the turning wheel of events. The wyrd appears as an intricate web linking seen and unseen worlds. The wyrd references Shakespeare's three witches (the weird sisters) in his Scottish play, who bear more than a passing resemblance to the classical Fates within Graeco-Roman mythology and the Fae in European folklore. All these characters share a common thread, the weaving and influencing of significant events. An appropriate analogy for working magic.

This web of the wyrd has come represent a typology of the flux and flow of the tides of magic. It encompasses all our possible experience, the events that have made us and contains all potentials of future outcomes. It's reach and influence is global and universal.

If we accept that everything in the universe connected, it is easy to recognise that everything is also in motion and subject to change. Even objects that appear to be stationary, are vibrating at various frequencies. When different oscillating things are close together for a time, they begin to resonate, correspond, and synchronize. This outcome is significant in both physics and magic. This 'spontaneous self-organisation' creates a flexible order in the universe, as everything manages and influences everything else. It explains how, against the odds, there is life in a universe that somehow 'holds together'. The interconnected nature of a moving universe may well be the reason how magic works. When an object is already in motion there is less frictional force opposing your push. An intentional 'tug' on the web of the wyrd through a well-cast sigil, may be all that is required to create change.

A further image of how magic works is provided by authors Janet Farrar and Gavin Bone in *Progressive Witchcraft* (2004). Within Norse mythology, Yggdrasil, the Holy Ash World Tree is believed to connect the Underworld to Heaven through its branches and roots representing the *axis mundi*, a line linking human experience to the underworld and heavenly realms. A similar tree is described in the Hindu Upanishads as '*a tree eternally existing, its roots aloft, its branches spreading below.*' The Great Tree is a universal icon found in many cultures acting as a guide for human consciousness. It often sets the storyline for an observation of human experience. Similar trees are found in the Shamanic, Egyptian, Sumerian, Toltec, Mayan, Celtic and traditions. In Jewish mysticism and later western esotericism, the tree of Life maps the journey through the Kabbalah. The jury is out on how the tree of the knowledge of good and evil in the Genesis story of the Fall, matches or mismatches these ideas, I suspect it all depends on interpretation.

The Web of the Wyrd interconnects and influences all things. It encompasses the Great Tree, which represents the Axis Mundi.
All of our past influences through ancestors and previous experience are brought into the present around the trunk of the tree. Our future choices are represented by the upward branches.

If these examples are a little too esoteric for your taste, consider a more natural interpretation. There exists a special relationship between trees and humans, as we both produce the gasses that enable the other to exist. They produce the oxygen that we need to breathe, and we produce carbon dioxide which trees breathe. Trees communicate with each other through underground networks of fungi that grow around their roots called mycorrhizal networks. Through this web of connection, trees share water and nutrients, and information about possible threats like disease, droughts, or insect attacks. It's an entirely beneficial arrangement for all parties.

In human experience, the underworld realms or roots can simply represent the genetic influence of long dead ancestors, equally branches reaching upwards symbolise our future choices. No profound occult explanations are required. Both the web of the wyrd and the great tree reveal an interconnected set of influences. Whether these models draw upon natural or supernatural forces is less significant than an expectation that magic works, in whatever way you picture it and however you anticipate it.

As you read this book, you are seeing words on pages, mildly aware of your environment, the things you need to do, and countless other thoughts and sensations, all present at one time. We are conscious beings, located in a world of experience. Maybe there really is a form of consciousness in everything. If this is so, all that differentiates the smallest subatomic atom from those that comprise your complex nervous system, is their configuration.

A meta-theory of consciousness allows for magic to flow between conscious intent and the subconscious mind, to inhabit and influence an 'experiencing universe'. Whatever conclusions we draw about how magic works (or even if we care) magic is not exclusively found in specific lodges, societies, or covens. It need not necessarily be practiced by correct or 'authorised' formulas, incantations, rituals, or exclusive belief systems. It is found by recognising, spinning, and influencing the thread connecting all these things. Thus, the weaver and the woven, are intrinsically joined.

# 11
# SIGILS AS PORTALS

*"Nothing I can see looks like an exit, so I'm making you into a door" - John Foxx*

A signature carries the authority of the signatory. Whilst this is becoming increasingly rare most legal documents still require one, even if it's in an electronic form. This authorises a course of action based upon the credit or status of the signatory. In a similar way sigils have been used to conjure spirits to aid the magician. These sigils are a representation of the essence of a particular entity, spirit, angel, or demon.

Sigil of Lilith — Sigil of Lucifer — Sigil of Astaroth

Many examples are drawn from historic grimoires, textbooks that contain magical techniques, often but not exclusively, influenced by Greco-Egyptian, Judeo-Christian, and Arabic magic. This subject, with its vast array of influences has recently received attention from many authors, including Jake Stratton-Kent and notably David Rankin in The Grimoire Encyclopaedia (2022). Many grimoires classify spirits or entities according to realm, form, or function, based on ideas about the structure of an ordered universe, reflecting the religious preference or cosmology of the day. Consequently archangels, the Virgin Mary and passages from the Bible are referenced alongside infernal legions of demons and their commanders.

It is helpful to clarify your own thinking when considering these ideas. Dualism, the belief that the world comprises of two opposing forces, has unduly influenced Western thought. Its observable within conflicting ideas about spirit and matter and what constitutes good and evil. It may well be compounded by ideas on 'spirituality' when this is worn as a badge of merit, favouring a detached asceticism over more earthly natural inclinations. Christianity, the dominant narrative in the West, has claimed that 'the fall' created a division of cosmic proportions. As a result, all nature and all metaphysical realms are divided by sin. Original angelic beings, now fallen from heaven, are recast as demons opposing God. This view has been revived by fundamentalist Christians and some New Age ideologies. It can be hard to tell them apart sometimes. This perspective or worldview can be critiqued for being overly simplistic and thus open to manipulation by 'gatekeepers', whether they are self-styled gurus, New Church apostles or media moguls. Invariably this binary narrative follows the same trajectory, those who agree with a particular view are 'on the side of angels' those who differ are 'possessed by demons.' Tragically, throughout history, these ideas have led to persecution and sadly are evident in contemporary American politics and other parts of the world.

Magic is an immanent or 'present' experience based on intent, however our connection within the web of the wyrd reveals a transcendent realm, sometimes appearing beyond our grasp. Congruence between the magician's will in the 'here and now' in an ever-expanding universe of multiple outcomes and influences, dramatically dissolves the final dualistic distinction between immanence and transcendence. Successful magic requires the suspension of binary beliefs, and if you can overcome prejudicial language, leads to working with entities variously called angels or demons. As a well-known Professor of History during a talk at the International Left-hand Path conference in 2020 noted.

> *"To evoke the spirits is to understand the cosmos and the freedom to walk the magic path, developing the way to suit the self. Today we have a great choice to pick from. Throughout history we have always adapted to our own needs. Remember, angels do not understand human needs, demons do".*

The concluding sentence makes a great point from Christian theology. Many sigils are concerned with obtaining results in everyday situations and meeting basic human requirements. Here an entity commonly called a demon can be very obliging.

If the idea of a robed ceremonial magician commanding angels and demons to fulfil their every wish doesn't appeal to you, relax, there is another way of using grimoires for sigil magic. A grimoire is a book of attributes, that contains information capable of creating change. In this respect anything can act as a grimoire, its value lies in its capacity to conjure images that speak to our conscious and unconscious minds. Antiquity, hidden secrets, and historical provenance carry their own charm, however contemporary cultural images also contain their own energy.

One of the most interesting examples of this was the formative influence of the American pulp science fiction magazines *Amazing Stories* and *Astounding* on Jack Parsons, at a time when both space travel and occult magic were considered fantasy fiction. Overcoming scientific prejudice, Parsons developed both, creating solid rocket fuel which would be later used by the NASA Space Program, whilst invoking Pan and Babalon in OTO temples and the Mojave Desert. Parsons saw no division between the human exploration of Space and magical inquiry into metaphysical realms. Today, Parsons, is regarded by many as the father of space travel. In his writings, particularly the essay *We are the Witchcraft* (1946), he presents a fascinating alternative to his English contemporary, Gerald Gardner.

Popular culture creates its own mythology. Consider the impact of a best-selling film, book, or TV series, with its publicity, merchandise, and subsequent spinoffs. Strong, well-developed characters with distinct personalities are both appealing and entertaining. They are designed as such for audiences to identify with them. Some of the best examples are flawed people with endearing traits that we can't help but admiring and wishing we that we possessed. An established narrative with diverse, often quirky characters can create a grimoire-like opportunity for magic and self-transformation.

In 2008 I became fascinated by the character of Patrick Jane from the TV series *The Mentalist*. Jane, played by Simon Baker, is a former psychic and con man, who ends up assisting the California Bureau of Investigation. It may not have possessed the most original of storylines, however the interaction between Jane as a civilian consultant and Teressa Lisbon the lead agent of the CBI, provided an amusing liminal dilemma. Jane's character pays more than a passing resemblance to a latter-day Sherlock Holmes, using observational skills, hypnosis, and sleight of hand to great effect, initially teasing the underlying question as to whether Jane was simply a reformed con artist or a genuine psychic. As the plot unfolded over several seasons, He denied any supernatural ability, yet used this reputation to his advantage. I have briefly worked as a platform healer but became uncomfortable with the opportunity to manipulate results without necessarily using psychic abilities, consequently, I felt some empathy towards him. Most of all I admired his relaxed non-confrontational approach to problem-solving and range of cold-reading skills. I adopted his style of drinking tea, reclining on a sofa whilst problem solving and found myself using the same phrases and downloaded the series theme tune as my phone ringtone. Obviously, I was never going to be as good-looking or afford to drive a vintage Citroen DS Pallas, but that wasn't the point. When confronted with a dilemma, I would ask myself, '*what would Patrick Jane do*'? It was an interesting, albeit highly subjective exercise.

In the excellent Pop Magic, occultist, producer and prolific comic book writer, Grant Morrison outlines the creation of a hypersigil, a collective of overlapping sigils expressed in a fictional, interactive narrative, in which he recreates his personality.

> *"The 'hypersigil' or 'supersigil' develops the sigil concept beyond the static image and incorporates elements such as characterization, drama, and plot. The hypersigil is a sigil extended through the fourth dimension. My own comic book series The Invisibles was a six-year long sigil in the form of an occult adventure story which consumed and recreated my life during the period of its composition and execution. The hypersigil is an immensely powerful and sometimes dangerous method for actually altering reality in accordance with intent. Results can be remarkable and shocking."*

Sigil magic facilitates the manipulation of internal and external realities, projecting our dreams and intentions into a lived experience so that it becomes a self-fulfilling prophecy. Few of us have the time or skills necessary for the type of complex sigil outlined by Morrison. Thankfully, there are simpler techniques that can be easily applied.

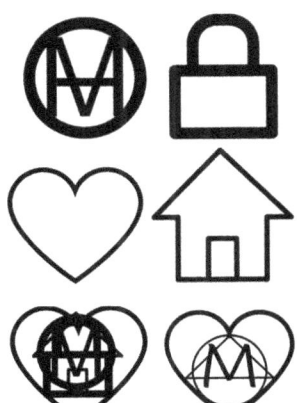

This example creates series of sigils aimed at Oli achieving his current life goals and moving forward in his life. The first statement is reduced and turned into a simple sigil, the remaining statements are represented pictorially and overlaid. The final sigil is then simplified.

**I am Oli. I am secure in my job.**
**I am loved by my partner.**
**My accommodation suits my growing needs.**

Sigils can bring real transformation, changing your life. In the same way that the square of Saturn provides the energy of discipline for the magician, the sigil of Lilith could be incorporated within a sigil to break free from oppression, particularly from a dominant male.

Lilith embodies the worst fears of male order, actively rejecting both patriarchal dominance and an alleged divine order for society. For this heinous crime she was forever demonised, cast out and held responsible for infanticide, the seduction of pious men and all acts of sedition. Lilith shares the same religious hatred shown to Jezebel and the Whore of Babylon in the Old and New Testaments of the Bible. Lilith is the ultimate antinomian icon.

The following sigil utilises three interrelated statements as affirmations.

**I am invincible.**

**You are as dust to me.**

**I stand in my own strength.**

They are reduced and overlaid on the sigil of Lilith, the image that 'speaks' to you can be turned into a sigil.

'I am invincible, you are as dust to me, I stand in my own strength'.

I am invincible you are as dust to me I stand in my own strength

**mnvcblyrdstgh**

mnvcblyrdstgh

**Overlay n** *over* **m**

**v** *over* **y**

**c** *over* **b**

**l** *over* **d**

**r** over **h**

**s** over **g**

Remaining letters **y b d h g t**

You could *mirror* **b** into **d**

In the examples below are the letters **y b d h g t** drawn into a sigil grid, overlayed onto the sigil of Lilith.

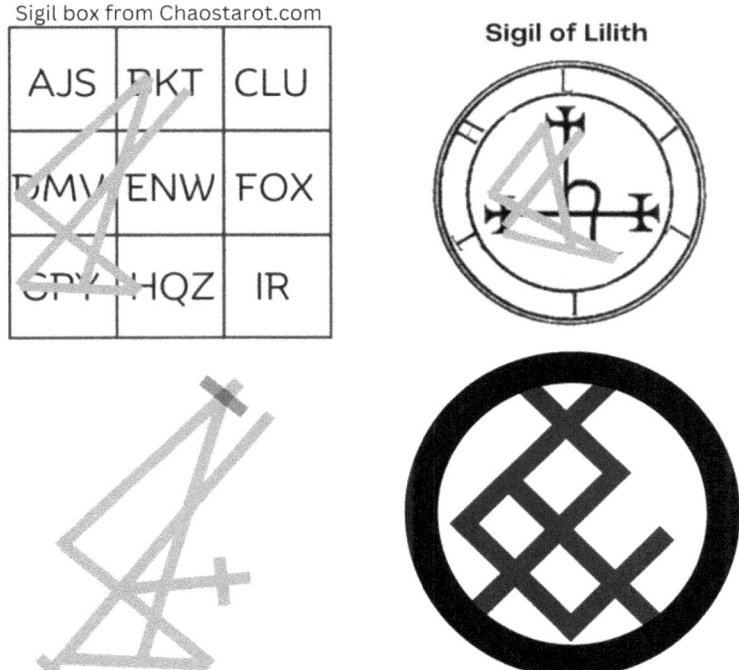

The three crosses stood out in my mind, so they were used as the basis for the final sigil, which was placed in a circle. Personally, I like to loop sections of an appropriate song in my head whilst casting sigils, it seems to work well. If you like your music loud and thrashy, I can thoroughly recommend *'Stay away (from me)'* by all-girl punk band Maid of Ace.

## A Simple Invocation technique

Throughout history culture has honoured deities and spirits for their qualities and attributes. It is possible to learn from and temporarily experience these first hand, entering a trance state and through invocation, achieving a brief possession by a spirit, to bring a particular aspect or quality to an individual. Precisely who is invoked is a matter of personal preference.

For example, someone who needs greater communication skills within business may benefit from encountering the Roman god Mercury. Similarly, the skill of an artist or craftsperson might be transformed through the Celtic god Lugh. Those wishing to find romantic love might seek an experience of the Greek goddess Aphrodite or the 'lusty' Pan. Take your pick, there are plenty of entities to choose from.

Obviously, this sort of activity should not be entered into without preparation and research, ideally having observed and worked with an experienced practitioner. As with all trance-work, it is important to ensure that you are in a good mental state and clear in your intention. Always exercise a healthy degree of caution and good old fashioned common sense.

Assuming this is the case, prepare yourself by clearly considering the qualities and potential impact of the entity you will invoke. This act aligns you or someone else with the entity being invoked. It is often easier to act as a portal or conduit by invoking into someone who desires these qualities, they too should be clear in their intention and in good mental health. The act of invocation carries a huge level of responsibility, so it is also helpful to include a third person who acts as an observer, situated slightly beyond your view, to witness to events as they unfold. Select a location that is a safe space for all involved and free from interruptions.

Many magicians enter a light trance by creating a sacred space, often by casting a circle. This both acts as an act of preparation and a place for encounter. Use whatever is your preferred approach. When you are ready, ensure you are in a light trance, but still aware of your surroundings. Stand facing the person being invoked into, who can hold or wear a sigil of the deity, (or a sigil representing their intention) being welcomed in. This acts as an anchor linking the entity to the person being invoked in.

Stand with your feet firmly placed on the ground, breathe deeply, smile in anticipation, and wait. This stage is important, I picture it like a surfer waiting in the ocean for the right wave to emerge. Timing is everything. When you sense its arrival, slowly raise your outstretched hands over the head of the person opposite you and invite the entity into them. Picture a wave gently breaking over them. You will probably sense a change take place straightaway; their expression may change, (apparently my eyes change colour) and as you feel this transformation, gradually bring your hands downwards, slowly tracing an outline a few inches around their body, until you are kneeling in front of them. Allow time for this process to take effect, it may cause a significant change in them, or it may be accompanied by a stillness and reassurance of the presence of the deity or spirit.

Wait until you are sure the job is done. Then thank the entity and ask them to leave the person. Ensure the person has come out of a trance, smile at them, and check they are OK. If they are a little groggy offer a drink or a snack. Close your space, usually by thanking and unwinding your circle. Allow sufficient time for grounding before embarking on any travel.

Magic involves a degree of risk-taking and uncertainty, these can be minimalised by good preparation and acting responsibly. Assuming all has gone well, the person concerned should notice a profound change in their lives. It may help if they write down their experience and create a sigil. You both may find it helpful to refer to the observer for additional information. Sometimes the person may wish to subsequently honour the entity through small acts of devotion. This is not uncommon, although you should ensure this doesn't become unduly obsessive.

# 12

# TRANCE SIGILS

*"Magical possession is both useful and enjoyable, if a little hair-raising at times"* - Phil Hine

The process of gnosis is highly useful in sigil construction, it acts as a technique to filter out conscious thought and carries the potential to manipulate our perceptions of reality. It creates a temporary lapse in rational thought, that opens the way for magic to occur. Austin Osman Spare described this emptying of the mind as 'vacuity'. It can be as simple as settling down and observing grasses waving in the wind, listening to waves, or watching as clouds cast moving shadows across a landscape. These examples provide a light trance experience that can be easily used as a prelude to sigil magic and to charge a sigil, emerging from this state releases it.

This process can be simple, for example entering a mild trance by sketching a repetitive border around your sigil. This can be a barely conscious act, particularly if you are prone to doodling. Alternatively, you could 'absentmindedly' add a flowing border of infinity symbols to charge your design. Phil Hine has developed this technique, which uses indifference, like Spare's vacuity to draw or replicate an existing sigil. This works well in meetings or lectures where only your presence is required, but only requires negligible contribution. Even terminal boredom creates opportunities for sigil magic.

Simple trance techniques include meditation and associated acts, like contemplation and yoga, charging occurs by simply picturing your sigil whilst in this state. You can mediate on a sigil before going to bed, so your unconsciousness mind charges it. My partner tried this, only to dream about their design changing and simplifying, at which point they woke up and drew the amended sigil, which subsequently became a tattoo.

Trance states can also be used to create or even discover a sigil. Many years ago, a friend and I created a sigil to help someone move forward in their magical development. Sitting opposite each other and stating our intention, we used a technique which involved passing energy between us and allowing it to increase in intensity until such a point we each drew it in to ourselves. At this point we turned opposite to each other and started to sketch our response. This was a combination of feelings and images, sounds, and symbols. They included quite random shapes, some easily recognisable, others less so. When we compared drawings, they shared some similarity. Both included a winged creature surrounding a patterned circle with a pentagram. It was an interesting experience, it felt like we had achieved something significant, even if you would expect witches to see pentagrams. The wings were more puzzling, as was a vague sound we both heard during the experience. The following morning, we left early to attend a conference in Glastonbury at which Janet Farrar and Gavin Bone were speaking. Unusually, they also had a small stall of jewellery, which contained unique designs and there to our surprise and amusement was our sigil, as a tiny silver pendant. Thankfully the artist had provided the description 'Minoan honeybee pendant based on a Bronze Age design found in Crete'. This explained the strange sound we heard the previous evening; magic always contains charming coincidences. The sigil was partially successful and the person it was designed for eventually moved on. The pendant has remained around my neck, occasionally lent to friends embarking upon difficult journeys.

Another variation of this is the creation of a sigil to represent and protect a group. These sigils are act like talismans, sometimes forming a totem for a coven. In this instance those present enter a trance through drumming with rhythmic dancing. As the energy rises, a series of questions are asked, and answers noted. For example, *what colour are you? What sound do you hear? What are you doing? What do you like?* Finally, *what is your name?* This works best done quickly, bypassing the need for thought or collusion with others, and with each person providing a one-word answer. In this case a replica model was made and carried into rituals and given offerings appropriate to its preferences.

Both these examples use a type of light trance or flow state, sometimes described as 'effortless attention'. In this state people become less self-critical of their contribution and more focused on a specific outcome, so it's particularly helpful in creating, charging, and releasing sigils.

Some approaches use sensory deprivation, for example fasting and sleeplessness to inhibit or bypass normal conscious thought and increase focus on a sigil. Obviously, this requires a level of time, commitment, and training to be effective. Other trance techniques to charge sigils include events that super-stimulate. These take an experience to a point of no return; at this point the sigil is naturally flipped from the conscious to the unconscious mind. Some Chaos magicians have cited examples such as bungee jumping or using extreme experiences of pain or anger. I'm not too sure any of these examples really appeal to me, that said, the secret is to discover techniques that work for you.

Most books on sigils reference orgasm as a good example, as its one most people have experienced. It's a straightforward way to charge and release a sigil. Whatever your feelings on this type of sigil magic, it works effectively and is considerably easier and quicker technique than many others. It may be easier to perform this alone, so that the focus is solely directed on the image of the sigil, rather than pleasing your partner. If you are working with someone else, the sigil can be drawn somewhere visible on each partner as a focal point during foreplay and orgasm. Remember to fix your attention on the sigil and nothing else. If you can master this, the sigil can be drawn somewhere where friction will rub out the design, during the natural course of events. This will both charge and ultimately release it. Only use water soluble ink unless you want a more permanent sigil. Alternatively, the sigil can be drawn, or traced over, using body fluids. During orgasm, and afterwards, you may experience spasms and physical tremors, followed by a silent, still bliss. This final feeling both mirrors and fulfils the final stage in the witches' pyramid – to be silent. It is also interesting to note the relationship of a post-orgasm temporary loss of consciousness, poetically referred to as '*la petite mort*' or 'little death'.

However, the penultimate experience of shaking is significant as an indicator of the ancient practice of seething. It is perhaps the oldest trance technique and found all over the world.

Seething often involves repetitive motions, swaying, and shaking, practiced by devout Jews at the Wailing Wall, Sufi mystics, magicians, devotees of Voodoo and Santería, as well as shamanic practitioners. Jan Fries in *Seidways* (1996) notes a natural relationship between seething and the process of fermentation, during which the action of frothing produces mead or beer. It's a useful analogy recognising a physical process of change, that often leads to a change in consciousness. Many examples of seething are derived from *Seiðr* or seidr, a form of Norse sorcery first practiced during the late Scandinavian Iron Age. It is largely concerned with shaping the future, so it aligns well with sigil magic. Often seidr involved a *Völva* or seer occupying a place of prominence or 'high seat' entering a trance to communicate with the spirits and give oracles. This technique bears some similarity to the '*Drawing Down the Moon*' ritual within Wicca. Personally, I believe this is central within this form of witchcraft and leads naturally to oracles of prophecy, like those of a Völva, rather than simply or mundanely reciting the Charge of the Goddess.

One of the most obvious examples of seething appeared in the Quaker and Shaker movements of the 17th and 18th centuries. This ecstatic fervour influenced the subsequent emergence of Pentecostal and Charismatic churches. Repetitive singing, rhythmic dancing, and involuntary physical convulsions, direct believers into a trance and sometimes to utter prophecy. It's not uncommon for worshipers to experience physical collapse or being 'slain in the spirit'. On several occasions in huge auditoriums, I witnessed several thousand people collapse like a vast Mexican wave. The most common feature of these churches is 'speaking in tongues' or glossolalia. In an ecstatic state, worshippers pray, or sometimes sing, using unknown languages. Very occasionally this may be interpreted by someone else. Rather than being a unique feature of Christianity, or 'a sign of a restored New Testament church', it is commonplace in ecstatic traditions in most religions.

Within traditional magic this practice resembles the use of 'barbarous tongues.' This can entail reciting ancient words whose original meaning may be lost or not understood but retain efficacy in magical workings. The infamous occultist Aleister Crowley described this technique in *Magick in Theory and Practice* (1929) as

> *"Long strings of formidable words which roar and moan through so many conjurations have a real effect in exalting the consciousness of the magician to the proper pitch."*

Undoubtedly this technique facilitates a change in consciousness, it also bears some similarity to the Norse practice of galdr or intoning runes. It is a powerful technique to charge sigils and one that I thoroughly recommend. It's fair to say, some people find this easier than others. Many of us were taught to think before we speak and generally this is good advice. However, this approach requires the opposite. In the first instance, it is easier to try this on your own and somewhere where you won't be overheard. Enter a light trance through whatever technique works best for you. Next picture your sigil (not your intention) and whilst continuing to focus on the image, allow random spontaneous syllables and sounds to form and say them out loud. You may find they form a natural rhythm. Vocalising is crucial, and *yes, it does get easier with practice*.

Several records of Seiðr imply the actual or figurative use of a cord as a snare or halter in a process of attraction, consistent with spinning the web of the wyrd. It bears some similarity to types of cord magic. This might take the form of fixing a focal point with a pole or staff and circling it with increasing intensity, so you are turning, and then spinning around the axis mundi, the centre of the web of the wyrd. You may recognise its similarities with casting a circle and *'drawing together the threads of the web of life'*. Within different forms of witchcraft, a measured pace whilst 'walking the round' or 'treading the mill' use a similar technique.

This circular movement naturally creates a trance state, so you could chant a sigil during this process. Alternately a sigil could be placed at the centre to charge and release it. If an actual pole is used, the sigil could be displayed prominently on it. In a group setting, participants could circle around with a cord attached to the pole, it might resemble a (sha)manic maypole dance. I worked in one group that used pole dancing to raise a cone of power and release magic via a portable pole that was fixed to the floor and ceiling. It was magically effective and a lot of fun.

Incidentally, as Fries notes, just prior to the French revolution, the Marquis de Puysegur, a disciple of the early hypnotist Mesmer, used an old elm tree, with ropes tied to its branches, as a trance-healing device. His patients took up the ropes and held hands, forming a circle, whilst he raised a magnetic current. As this flowed around the circle those present started to sway rhythmically, once a subject convulsed, they were removed from the circle, which was resealed. They were placed in a somnambulistic or waking sleep state. The Marquis would gently question them about their illness and its causes, asking them for solutions to heal their condition. In his day this was a controversial approach, however recently, his contribution has been acknowledged by academics in influencing hypnotic techniques used in mainstream psychoanalysis and psychotherapy.

Another aspect of seething is breath control, not as we have seen in earlier chapters as a form of meditation leading to calm, but as an energising technique. I experienced this whilst practicing yoga as 'double breathing'. This is rhythmic breathing consisting of a rapid inhale through the nostril, immediately followed by a much deeper breath. This results in a super oxygenation trance, creating an incredible feeling of euphoria. It's a great way to charge a sigil. On two occasions I experienced an extraordinary out of body experience that confirmed my belief that my consciousness will continue in some way beyond physical death.

There are several versions of this technique, and I would strongly recommend you find a suitably qualified teacher to ensure it is done safely before you use it to cast a sigil.

Whenever you use trance to create, charge and release sigils, fully ensure the technique is suited to your physical and mental health.

# 13
# CROSSROADS SIGILS

*"At the borders of liminal space, someone or something waits, perhaps to interrupt our comfort or make a deal"*
*- JA*

A crossroads is one of the most interesting places to cast sigils. Magic can be observed through the intersection of the world tree and our present experience. By creating a magical working space or casting a circle and invoking cardinal points or elemental quarters, a further crisscrossing of pathways emerges. At this crossroads there is great potential for change and for many people it is the obvious place to a cast a sigil. However, a physical place, at the fork in the roads where paths cross, equally offers the possibilities of otherworldly encounters.

Janus

The Romans had different words for crossroads; *bifrons*, *trifrons* and *quadrofons* (two, three and four ways) each with attendant deities.

Janus is a bifron doorkeeper god who oversees transitions and gives his name to January.

Perhaps the most well-known is the triple-visaged trifron Diana Triva and the Greek goddess Hekate.

In ancient Greek and Roman culture, the responsibility for national and civic protection lay with elected representatives performing the appropriate state ceremonies. The well-being and protection of families and smaller communities rested with individual households enacting the appropriate offerings and rites. The festival of Compitalia honoured the household Lares or spirits by leaving offerings at the places where two or more roads crossed. The further 'out of town' you lived, the higher the level of risk from robbery, attack, and disruption from unruly spirits. Consequently, crossroads at the edges of human settlement were considered dangerous places, where malign spirits would dwell. Shrines were erected at the crossing of the ways to protect crops and used within seasonal agricultural rites to ensure a good harvest. These shrines acted as watchtowers, some were designed to face the four compass points, the seasonal rituals conducted there may well prefigure some aspects of the modern pagan Wheel of the Year.

The malevolent, negative nature of crossroads was continued by the Church, who buried criminals, suicides, and witches at crossroads. These were often boundary markers between parishes, far from the sanctuary of consecrated land. This created a literal no-man's land beyond clerical jurisdiction. Crossroads also marked wastelands used as general rubbish tips and seen as harbingers of illness. These practices merged with the belief that at crossroads the spirits of those buried there would become perpetually lost as if in a maze and confused as to which way to travel back to the village. Interestingly if you visit Creswell Crags in Nottinghamshire there is a spirit maze stone designed to trap malevolent entities.

The crossroads simultaneously became a mysterious 'go to' place for those seeking magic for healing and encounter and a dangerous 'no go' area for those in fear for their moral souls. In Malvern, until relatively recently, whenever a coffin was carried a cemetery along a 'corpse way' passed over a crossroad, the pallbearers would stop and exchange positions at the corners of the bier to prevent harm befalling them.

The intersection of tracks is significant within many religions, who have specific deities who guard the crossroads. Within Vodou and Quimbanda, practitioners draw symbols or veves in the earth to attract and honour crossroads deities and present them with requests. These symbols function in a similar way to traditional magical sigils.

**Veve Legba**  **Veve Ogum**

Papa Legba is a Vodou loa associated with the crossroads and doorways, where among other things, he functions as an intermediary between human and the spirit realms. Ogum fulfils a similar role in Quimbanda as Orisha at the crossroads.

Nicholaj de Mattos Frisvold notes in *Craft of the Untamed* (2011),

> *"The idea of the crossroad as an inter-dimensional portal has been integrated into Vodou both from French sorcery and African cosmologies. The crossroad is understood from mutually enriching angles."*

It is this co-operative feature of crossroads that offer the greatest benefits. Where paths intersect, journeys can change course and perhaps the help of another can be sought. There are plenty of mythological examples of 'deals done' where paths cross, for example, the legendary Faust met Mephistopheles at the Crossroads and exchanged his soul for wisdom and fortune. Musicians frequently feature in similar narratives. In 1935 Robert Johnson, a struggling musician, met a tall dark man at a crossroads in the Mississippi Delta, who tuned his guitar and returned it to Johnson, who subsequently gains fame for his newfound guitar skills. The Rock and Roll Hall of Fame described Johnson as *"the first ever rock star"*. Interestingly, musicians and artists frequently feature in crossroads encounters.

Arguably, there is always a price to be paid for such benefits, Faust eventually falls foul of his deal, Johnson dies from poisoning, probably by a jealous husband, three years after his crossroads encounter. If these are understood solely as morality tales, then the culture of the day determines the interpretation or validity of such encounters.

This is evident during the 11th Century, the clerical homily De Falsis Deis denounces the crossroads veneration of the god Mercury.

> *"At crossroads they offered sacrifices to him...all through the devil's teaching. This false god was honoured among the heathens of the day, and he is also called the name Odin in the Danish manner."*

The prohibition of crossroads encounters permeates church teachings, regional entities like the Germanic Der Teufel and significant deities such as Mercury/Odin are strategically recast as in league with, or the devil himself. It is a difficult taxonomy to unravel, and a theme that has provided authors and film-makers plenty of scope to develop. Not surprisingly, this has led some to avoid working at the crossroads. However, for those who understand the value of knowledge, willing, daring, and silence - these locations provide their own reward.

In traditional witchcraft, the character most likely to appear at the crossroads is known by many names, simply (and rather obliquely) referred to as 'the man in black'. Paradoxically, this figure is neither exclusively male nor human. They can appear in many forms, sometimes as a black dog, crow, serpent, or horned goat. Modern witchcraft has been quick to distance itself from any association with the devil and although the 'man in black' is not easily dismissed as a simple manifestation of the Christian devil, this often-overlooked figure represents the antithesis of a religious hierarchy that divides and diminishes human, animal, and spirit realms. 'He' is the enigmatic facilitator of chance and change. Crossroads are by their nature a non-binary place of challenge and intersectional experience. Sigil casting at the crossroads is a valuable experience, whether within the confines of a magical space or circle, or a literal, physical fork in the roads. The following example is adaptable in both instances.

The crossroads can provide an opportunity to acquire a new skill or develop and hone an existing one. Rather than physically taking a guitar, artist's easel or share portfolio, (or whatever else 'floats your boat') to a fork in the roads, you can simply include a graphic representation of it within your sigil.

Carefully consider your intention, write out several versions and gradually pare it down, so that it completely and perfectly reflects your true desire. Now turn it into a sigil using your preferred method. If you have collected soil or dust from a crossroads or a graveyard, you can draw your sigil in spit or blood and sprinkle it over the design. You can also incorporate a shape within your sigil that resembles the crossroads you are using.

You should select a location where you won't be disturbed, but that doesn't unduly endanger your safety. There are differing views on when you should cast your sigil, a new moon would be appropriate, however at night, a full moon in a clear sky should remove the need for additional light, which attracts too much attention. So be guided by your own knowledge and intuition.

As you approach your chosen destination on foot, walk slowly and purposefully, and focus on your intent. Avoid using peripheral vision at this stage (as if you are wearing a mask). If you are working indoors simply picture this as a meditative journey.

*When you arrive, make a suitable offering for the land at the crossroads. If you are in doubt as to what this should be, pour a small amount of strong drink out (this seems to work well whether inside or outside).*

*Stand, sit, (or imagine yourself) at the middle of the crossroads, holding your sigil and wait. You are at the intersection of all possibilities, crossroads are inter-dimensional places, where all is fluid. Narrow your eyes, further reducing your gaze and prepare for your encounter. You may sense the presence of someone or something quite quickly.*

*If you are doing this as a meditation, you can picture an entity moving slowly with intent simultaneously towards you down each path of the crossroads. As they converge, place your sigil on the ground and leave an offering, maybe a gold coin, but ideally a biodegradable gift.*

*Sometimes the 'man in black' appears wearing horns, between which burns a flame, guiding the seeker in an alternative direction and down an unseen path. If this occurs, pay particular attention to its meaning for you. If you are working outside, immediately bury your sigil. Stand and blink, then take several steps backwards, before turning around and returning home. If you are working inside, simply burn your sigil.*

*You may wish to make a subsequent payment, (other than a symbolic offering, like a gold coin) to conclude and release you from your encounter. Consider a donation to an associated charity that is in keeping with your request or any organisation that protects wildlife. This effectively concludes and 'seals the deal', absolving you any from any further obligation in this transaction ('to keep silent').*

There are other opportunities for using a sigil at the centre of a crossroads.

There are occasions when we can feel restricted in achieving our goals, as if something is thwarting our actions. This can be very frustrating and lead to a sense of discouragement. I first encountered this technique in *Modern Magick* (2011) by Donald Michael Kraig and adapted it for sigil casting at the crossroads.

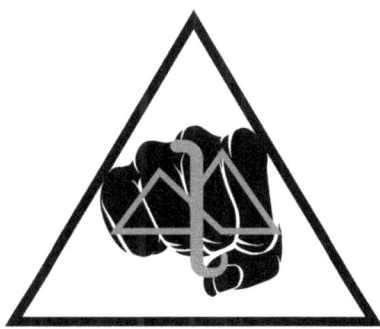

Ideally you should use a strongly phrased intention, for example, 'I am successful in all I do', reduced, condensed, and encapsulated in a triangle.

Locate a crossroads where at least two paths converge, creating four directions. Alternately, use a magic circle with cardinal points (North, South, East, and West).

Stand in your chosen location and close your eyes and become aware of your other senses. Begin to slowly pivot round in a circle, as you do this be open to any unusual sensory experience. This could be an increase or decrease of heat, sense of smell, or anything out of the ordinary that indicates a particular direction. Once you have determined this, stop, face that direction, and open your eyes. Stand tall, with your feet firmly on the ground and visualise your sigil glowing or pulsating in the middle of your forehead.

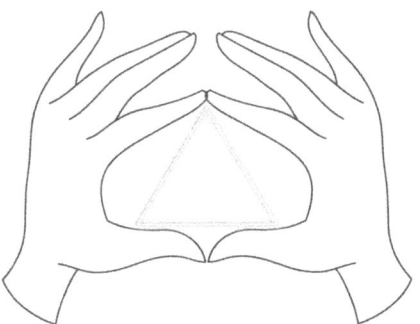

Bring your hands up to surround your shining sigil, with your hands flat so your thumbs meet just above your eyebrows and your fingers meet to form a triangle around your sigil.

Take a deep breath and step forward with one foot, and exhale fully, pushing your hands forward and thrusting your sigil out to achieve its goal. You can use this technique to cast a sigil anywhere.

# 14
# SIGILS AS SENTIENT BEINGS

*"If the land is poisoned, witchcraft must respond"*
*- Peter Grey*

In 2014 I experienced two traumatic events; these were to transform my approach to both sigils and magic. In January, my beloved mentor and valued friend, Maureen Wheeler, passed over after a short period in hospital. It was, to use a well-worn cliché, the end of an era. The knowledge that invariably all things must change, gradually led to a realisation that at this crossroads, I needed to change too.

In June I attended a conference in Reading, ostensibly to accompany my friend Vikki Bramshaw, who was speaking there. The drive there gave us the opportunity to reminisce about Maureen and the impact she had on our lives. Almost by chance, I wandered into a talk given by Peter Grey, entitled '*Rewilding Witchcraft*' and softly spoken words of admonishment and challenge struck a painful chord. I didn't like what he said and almost regretted attending, yet I couldn't help but feel he was making valid points. I suspect I was not alone in this.

Sigils are, for the most part, simple shorthand expressions of intent, designed, charged, released, and forgotten, so that their influence flows to accomplish change. However, they can be used to create a considerably greater impact than a singular wish. A sigil can be the precursor to a much larger event. As ideas about chaos magic have evolved, concepts within traditional magical practice have been reworked, remixed, and incorporated to great effect.

Most records of magic include the creation of a symbolic or actual being, imbued with life, to further the wishes of the magician. It bears similarity to the idea of a black robed magician summoning a demon with a request, yet differs in respect of provenance, in this case, the 'being' is literally created out of nothing.

Perhaps the most famous is the Golem, a figure within Jewish folklore. In the Middle Ages, texts from the Sefer Yetzirah described techniques to animate a figure of clay, using a mystical shem or name of G-d, written down and placed within the mouth of the clay effigy. Unlike a fith fath or poppet which usually represents an existing individual, the Golem represents an unformed being made from dust (not unlike Adam in the Genesis mythology) which is then brought to life. The Golem takes on characteristics and volition as instructed by the magician.

Within modern magic, this process can take the form of an evolution of distinct transitions, from sigil to servitor and possibly to egregore. Kenneth Grant, commenting on the writings of Spare, outlines this approach:

> *"By a form of Delphic Oracle involving the use of sigils and by intruding a sigil into the subconsciousness, it is able to think for us, and, if the sigil resumes a query concerning some future event, will breed from its own sentiency the true child of its symbolic parts."*

Consequently, a well-constructed sigil contains the potential for independent sentient activity. This is a very interesting idea.

A sigil may fulfil the role of a servitor acting on behalf of the magician, within clearly defined parameters. This might be to protect the boundaries of a property or community. It could function as a roving entity, to alert the magician when they are being talked about, particularly in a negative way. Servitors are useful to the magician.

A servitor is a super-sigil, its realm of activity is defined within its inception. For example, you might wish to create a servitor to bring you good luck. It could be initially designed as a sigil using your preferred method. You may wish to include specific limitations, for example, '*good luck that benefits me, but not at the expense of, or detriment, to anyone else*'. This can be further improved on by attaching corresponding associations you have with good fortune, expressions of how you feel when particularly lucky, or references to previous instances of serendipity. 'Sensation thinking' and codifying this within sigils is a valuable magical technique.

You should uniquely name and embed your sigil within a specific object. This works well if your servitor operates near its location. Alternatively, embed your sigil into a visualised being. Be totally creative, describing their appearance and personality, in a way that you can easily picture and communicate with them. Write out and read a statement of intent or mandate to birth them by creating a simple ritual. Servitors, by their nature have a limited lifespan, so as you create one, also include a process for their demise. This part is important.

Regularly remind your servitor by name, of your expectations and your relationship to them. You might want to 'raise a glass to them' or honour them in a particular action, as a regular activity. This will strengthen your connection to the servitor and your outcome.

The next stage of developing an egregore provided, in part, an actionable solution to the challenge to me presented at the start of the chapter.

**"As the man in black gazed on, Rome was reduced to ash".**

The crossroads I faced in 2014 related to the passing of an old order. Peter Grey in *Rewilding Witchcraft* rightly critiqued the tendency in contemporary witchcraft to favour social acceptance over radical, socially transformative, magical practice:

> *"How tame we have become. How polite our witchcraft. In our desire to harm none we have become harmless. We have bargained to get a seat at the table of the great faiths to whom we remain anathema. How much compromise have we made in our private practice for the mighty freedom of being able to wear pewter pentagrams in public, at school, in our places of employment".*

Grey continues making the following statement.

> *"I will not be part of this process, because to do so is to be complicit with the very forces that are destroying all life on earth. It is time for witchcraft not to choose, but to remember which side it is on in this struggle".*

His bleak environmental forecast was, in 2014, a challenging concept. Grey detailed the global demise of the four elements, honoured and welcomed in a magic circle, concluding each with the traditional greeting of *'hail and welcome'*.

Over the following four years, I struggled with the existential threat of the demise of all the things I valued, and the apparent impotence of my magical practice in halting this decline. Research confirmed much of Grey's findings and despite this, there seemed little will within Government or the media to promote a solution.

## The Leveller

In some way, I felt I had to act, or feel fraudulent in my beliefs. My solution was to create a sigil to highlight inactivity surrounding climate crisis and to create an entity that would *'level the injustice in the land'*. This carried more than a passing reference to the popular people's movement of the late 15th and early 16th century, that levelled hedges and walls to protest the enclosures acts which restricted access to the land, a right previously held by commoners.

 The Leveller sigil began life in a condensed form, simply LVR. As I played with these letters a recurring shape emerged that resembled a bridge. Bridges have long been considered magical liminal spaces, linking realms, and carrying ideas. Whether the bridge carries people, cars, trains or allows the flow of water, it facilitates movement and, in this case, provides energy for the growth of the thoughtform expressed through the sigil.

This proved to be significant as both a symbol of connection, allowing the passage of ideas, but also as the location for the sigil. Early in December 2018, I outlined my plans at an occult conference where the Leveller sigil was brought to life by chanting.

The sigil was subsequently chalked at the base of bridges across the South Coast, in fact anywhere where there was movement, this continued the charging process. These included motorway bridges, aqueducts, pedestrian bridges, even a wooden footbridge only really used by cattle and New Forest ponies. The most interesting were bridges connecting islands to mainland, as they had motion over the bridge, but also tidal energy flowing beneath. The were also the most dangerous to access, being covered in wet, slippery seaweed. The Leveller sigil was thrown from cars whilst travelling under or over bridges and remotely projected on Westminster bridge in London.

By the end of that year, a second aspect of bridges was actioned. In European folklore, bridges are guarded by Trolls who require payment for crossing the bridge, this idea generates the growth of the sigil via a 'troll toll' across the bridge into something more powerful. The 'role of the troll' was to act as a midwife, birthing the Leveller as a totally independent entity or egregore.

I wryly describe this process as *'Pinochean magic'*, a word play on Enochian Magic, which included spirit invocations and the development of watchtower guardians, developed by John Dee and Edward Kelley in the 16th century. The Leveller was created to watch over the land and expose lies perpetrated by oil corporations colluding with governments, and the owners of the media, who for vested interest largely ignore, refute, or play down the impact of climate crisis.

Most sigils are secret, known and then forgotten by the magician until they reach fruition. The construction of a sigil and its transformation into an egregore, had become a more public affair. I was often asked how we would know if our working had been successful. I wasn't entirely sure of the answer.

Egregores occupy an interesting space in occult thought. The mystical Jewish text, *The Book of Enoch* (300-200 BCE), implies these are 'watchers', original angelic beings who keep a wary eye on human activity. Other examples of egregores reference a non-physical entity that emerges from 'communities of intention' (see chapter 10). These sentient forces reflect and, in some way, direct the collective will or 'hive mind' of a particular group. The most recent definition locates an egregore as an independent entity that arises from the collective work of several magicians. Given the variation within these ideas, I felt the Leveller ticked several boxes.

Around the time of the Leveller's inception, two related events occurred. In Sweden a schoolgirl began a strike protesting environmental destruction; and a group of scientists and academics convened a new environmental movement, based upon an hourglass sigil. Over the following years both have become a global phenomenon, gaining huge support and criticism, the later often from governments and press barons.

These events were way beyond any single activity, and if the Leveller played a minuscule role in a much greater whole, I am thankful to all those who helped. In this respect, the Leveller functioned more as the third definition of egregore.

Within movements for social change, we can observe a similar effect to shoaling and perhaps even robofish. Magic of this nature can be best described as a 'murmuration', reflecting the amazing, synchronized patterns of starlings in flight, and in another sense, the complaints raised by many voices, perhaps describing the second definition of egregore.

I very much doubt that humanity will succeed in significantly halting environmental collapse or the obscene excesses of capitalism with the gross social inequality it engenders. I hope that some of the extremes of these can be curtailed through magic and protest.

Perhaps the intervention of the original definition of egregore, as external watcher, observing and waiting to act, is required.

As we continue within uncertain times, the magician remains both captivated by the laughter of the land and constrained by its lament.

As Gordon White notes:

> *"Magic is always the last resort of those who refuse to give up hope."*

# BIBLIOGRAPHY

William S. Burroughs - *The Doing Easy* (1973) extract from *Exterminator!*, Viking Press Books

Genevieve von Petzinger - *The First Signs* (2016), Simon and Schuster

Eliphas Levi - *Transcendental Magic* (1854 & 1856) modern edition published (1979), Rider

Paul Huson - *Mastering Witchcraft* (1970), G P Putnam's Sons

Dion Fortune - *The Sea Priestess* (1935), Inner Light Publishing Co.

Janet & Stuart Farrar - *A Witches' Bible* (1981), Robert Hale

Rhyd Wildermuth - *The Secret of Crossings* (2022), Gods & Radicals Press

Unknown - *Rasa'il* (10th Century CE)

Grant Morrison – 'Pop Magic' (extract from) *Book of Lies: The Disinformation Guide to Magick and the Occult* (2008) Ed Richard Metzger, Disinformation Company The Limited, T.H.E.

Unknown - *Hermes Trismegistus* ($2^{nd}$–$3^{rd}$ Century BCE)

Dave Lee - *Chaotopia* (2nd ed 2006), Mandrake

Gordon White - *Chaos Protocols* (2020), Llewellyn

Unknown - *Poetic Edda* (late 13th Century)

Donald Michael Kraig - *Modern Magick* (2010), Llewellyn

Mary Stewart Relfe - *The New Money System 666* (1982), Montgomery, Ala. : Ministries, Inc

Julian Jaynes - *The Origin of Human Consciousness in the Breakdown of the Bicameral Mind* (1976), HarperCollins

Graham Harvey - *Listening People Speaking Earth* (1997), Hurst & Company

Brian Bates - *The Way of Wyrd* (2004), Hay House

Janet Farrar & Gavin Bone - *Progressive Witchcraft* (2004), New Page

David Rankin - *The Grimoire Encyclopaedia* (2022), Hadean Press

Jack Parsons – '*We are the Witchcraft*' (1946) excerpt from *Freedom is a Two-Edged Sword* ed. Heymeneus Beta (William Breeze) (1990), Oriflamme

Jan Fries - *Seidways* (1996), Mandrake

Aliester Crowley - *Magick in Theory and Practice* (1929), Lecram

Nicholaj de Mattos Frisvold - *Craft of the Untamed* (2011), Mandrake

Ælfric of Eynsham - *De Falsis Deis* (late 10th century)

Peter Grey – '*Rewilding Witchcraft*' (extract from) *Brazen Vessel* (2019), Scarlet Imprint

Unknown - *The Book of Enoch* (300-200 BCE)

Kenneth Grant - *Austin Osman Spare: An introduction to his psycho-magical philosophy*, Volume IV of the Carfax Monographs

Websites:

chaostarot.com

runesoup.com

www.ingramcontent.com/pod-product-compliance
Lightning Source LLC
Chambersburg PA
CBHW041318110526
44591CB00021B/2826